CAR

Backwards into
the Future

Meditations on the
Letter to the Hebrews

by

John FitzGerald, O.Carm.

**With a guide to Lectio Divina
by Carlos Mesters, O.Carm.**

TYPOGRAPHIA
STI ALBERTI

Saint Albert's Press / Gwasg S. Albert

Cover illustration: *The Risen Christ*, painting by Adam Kossowski in the Rosary Way at the Carmelite Shrine of Saint Jude, Whitefriars, Faversham, Kent.

Edited by Johan Bergström-Allen.

Design & typeset by Ing. Jakub Kubů, Prague, Czech republic, on behalf of Karmelitánské nakladatelství s.r.o., Thákurova 3, 160 00 Praha 6, Czech Republic.

Printed by ERMAT Praha s.r.o., Czech Republic.

Saint Albert's Press would like to thank Mr. Anthony Packer, Fr. John Owen, Fr. Carlos Mesters, O.Carm., and Fr. Míceál O'Neill, O.Carm. for their assistance in the production of this book.

First published 2005 by Saint Albert's Press.

Saint Albert's Press
Whitefriars, 35 Tanners Street,
Faversham, Kent, ME13 7JN, U.K.

ISBN: 0-904849-30-9

[1] Let mutual love continue. [2] Do not neglect to show hospitality to strangers, for by doing that some have entertained angels without knowing it. [3] Remember those who are in prison, as though you were in prison with them; those who are being tortured, as though you yourselves were being tortured. [4] Let marriage be held in honour by all, and let the marriage bed be kept undefiled; for God will judge fornicators and adulterers. [5] Keep your lives free from the love of money, and be content with what you have; for he has said, 'I will never leave you or forsake you.' [6] So we can say with confidence, 'The Lord is my helper; I will not be afraid. What can anyone do to me?' [7] Remember your leaders, those who spoke the word of God to you; consider the outcome of their way of life, and imitate their faith. [8] Jesus Christ is the same yesterday and today and forever.
(Hebrews 13: 1-8)

CONTENTS

FOREWORD

The author of the *Letter to the Hebrews* wrote around 70 A.D. to a community of Jews who had recently become Christian, reminding them that 'the Word of God is living and active, sharper than any two-edged sword' *(Hebrews* 4:12). As pastors of the Catholic Church in Wales we commend these gentle meditations on that *Letter* written by Father John FitzGerald, a Carmelite friar, to everyone who sincerely wishes to make that Word of God, as it is found in the Bible, an active presence in their lives.

As a Carmelite, Father John draws on one of the most ancient traditions of Christian spirituality. This work is complemented by Father Carlos Mesters whose concise but masterful *Introduction to Lectio Divina* explains how for centuries individuals and communities have regularly pondered God's Word as a source of strength in daily life, and tells us how we can join them in drinking from the crystal fountain of holy scripture. Father John's words as he reflects on the *Letter to the Hebrews* draw deeply from these sources. They are sensitively chosen, reflecting his scholarship, the authentic tradition he is transmitting, and his own poetic skill. As he tells us in his introduction, these meditations were first published in the Welsh language. Now translated into English by his own hand, they faithfully reproduce his sharply honed and active engagement with the Word of God.

Catholic Wales is indebted to Father John for bringing this gift to a broader audience in the much larger English-speaking Catholic community. He has himself been remarkable for his labour in making the cultural tradition of Wales his own, not simply as a possessor but as a contributor. He is well aware how deeply Catholic the Christian tradition of Wales was from the early centuries. If we are to realise the insistent recall to Christian unity which is now demanded of us we will do well to ensure that we too can be complimented on our knowledge of the Bible, which is indivisible in its ultimate significance from the Eucharist and the visible community of the Church as the Body of Christ.

Father John explains in these meditations that the Church which received the *Letter to the Hebrews* was a disillusioned community whose members had suffered for their faith as followers of Jesus Christ. Our circumstances are different, but like those early believers, we too can become disillusioned and mesmerised by the immediate demands and requirements of a disbelieving society. It is, therefore, a timely reminder to Christians in Wales at the beginning of the Third Millennium that we too have here 'no lasting city, but are looking for the city that is to come' (*Hebrews* 13:14). That city is the Kingdom of God, and in order to build it in this, our own part of the world, we must be deeply attentive to the Scriptures, and their excellent news of Jesus Christ.

Whether you are already familiar with reading the Bible, or whether it is something you have never really done before, we encourage you to encounter the Word of God in a renewed way this year with the help of this book. These reflections have been prepared as Lenten reading for individuals, groups, and parishes across our dioceses. They will help you to appreciate the *Letter to the Hebrews* not simply as a piece of literature written nearly two thousand years ago, but as a profound affirmation of the timeless Christian values of hope, conversion, discipline, forgiveness, generosity, hospitality, and love.

These virtues are still active, but they need cultivation in our lives. For this reason we earnestly hope that you will spend some time, and not only during this Lent, to use Father John's reflections in this book as 'solid food' (*Hebrews* 5:14) for nourishing your own relationship with the God who, in Jesus Christ, has become 'one like us'.

+ Most Rev. Peter D. Smith, LLB, JCD
Archbishop of Cardiff

+ Right Rev. Mark Jabalé, OSB
Bishop of Menevia

+ Right Rev. Edwin Regan
Bishop of Wrexham

Ash Wednesday, 9th February, 2005

ABOUT THE AUTHORS

John FitzGerald joined the Carmelite Order in 1942. As a Carmelite friar he has long served our Catholic community in Wales, and his own religious family, as a pastor and a scholar.

He first came to Wales in January 1940 when he began studying at the Junior Seminary, St. Mary's College, Castell Brychan, Aberystwyth. There he met Saunders Lewis who was then teaching Welsh to the boys who might later be ordained as priests in Wales. Greatly inspired by this teacher, he went on to study the language and literature of Wales at University College Dublin, under Professor John Lloyd Jones, who also directed his attention toward the Classics. Following his ordination to the priesthood he was sent by the Order, in 1952, to the Gregorian University in Rome for post-graduate study in theology. He then went to Cambridge University to continue reading Classics.

The Carmelites next sent him to Tre-gib, Llandeilo, where they then had a school. He taught there until the school moved to Cheltenham in 1958. Father John was appointed to remain at Tre-gib to teach philosophy to students within the Order. In 1964 he was appointed by the Order as Catholic Chaplain at the University of Wales, Aberystwyth, and was to work in the town for the next forty years. In 1970, he became a Lecturer in Philosophy at the university, teaching principally in the Welsh language, and when he retired from this position in 1993 he returned to the Chaplaincy where he continued to work until 2004. At present he is prior of the Carmelite community at Llanelli.

Father John has been notable in his work as a spiritual director, and for his scholarship in the sacred languages. He has also given unstinting attention to the cause of the Welsh community and its culture. He has lectured and published widely and written poetry in the Welsh language. Father John is a supporter of the National Eisteddfod, and was a member of the Joint Supervisory Committee of the New Welsh Bible from its inception. He was joint Editor of *Llyfr Offeren y Sul* (the Missal for Sundays and Holy days), and is Editor of *Y Cylchgrawn Catholig,* a journal which sensitively represents Catholic scholarship and spirituality in the native language of Wales, and is a contributor to *Efrydiau Athronyddol* a journal of philosophical study.

* * *

Carlos Mesters is a Carmelite friar from Holland, and one of his Order's leading experts on reading the Bible. His approach to *Lectio Divina*, the prayerful reading of the holy scriptures, arises from his experience of working for many years with 'base communities' in Brazil. He now lives in Rome as the Carmelite Order's Councillor General for Latin America.

BACKWARDS INTO THE FUTURE: MEDITATIONS ON THE *LETTER TO THE HEBREWS*

Introduction

'GOD knows who wrote *Hebrews*', said Origen: all the same, the book is Scripture, the Word of God speaking through an anonymous but learned and able author.

It is a fascinating and eloquent composition: it starts with the message that the 'many and various ways' of God's speaking to his people of old are now caught up, fulfilled, and surpassed in his speaking to us in his son Jesus; and goes on to use all the resources of the old scriptures to present the significance of the Son. On the one hand, the old rituals and remedies for sin are now void, superseded by the suffering, death, resurrection and ascension of the Son, because of who he is and what he has done for us, (chapters 1-10). Yet, on the other hand, the life of faith which was lived in the presence of God can be traced in the old (indeed the oldest) traditions (chapters 11-12), and continues to be an example for us. For us too, there is quiet light on the inner meaning of Mass and Eucharist.

This little book started life in Welsh in 1994 in the series *O Ddydd i Ddydd*. It was not and is not meant as a commentary, although there is an element of commentary here and there. The purpose is to offer the reader (who is willing to work at it) some help towards engaging bit by bit with the text of *Hebrews* in meditation and prayer. Whilst it is meant as a help to *lectio divina*, and not a substitute for it, an introduction to *lectio divina*, by my Carmelite confrere Carlos Mesters, is appended to the book to help the reader along the way.

In order to facilitate reflection, the text of the *Letter to the Hebrews* is reproduced in its entirety, chapter by chapter. The text and quotations are taken from the New Revised Standard Version (anglicized edition), without insisting that readers may not use another version of their choice. I give frequent cross-references to other places in scripture, because I myself find that a help; of course one needs to remember that there may be different contexts to sayings that initially look similar. What is important is that the reader daily approaches the throne of grace (*Hebrews* 4:16), which is more important than working through the whole book line by line.

And when it is opportune, please pray for

John FitzGerald, O.Carm.

Letter to the Hebrews

Chapter 1

[1] Long ago God spoke to our ancestors in many and various ways by the prophets, [2] but in these last days he has spoken to us by a Son, whom he appointed heir of all things, through whom he also created the worlds. [3] He is the reflection of God's glory and the exact imprint of God's very being, and he sustains all things by his powerful word. When he had made purification for sins, he sat down at the right hand of the Majesty on high, [4] having become as much superior to angels as the name he has inherited is more excellent than theirs. [5] For to which of the angels did God ever say, 'You are my Son; today I have begotten you'? Or again, 'I will be his Father, and he will be my Son'? [6] And again, when he brings the firstborn into the world, he says, 'Let all God's angels worship him.' [7] Of the angels he says, 'He makes his angels winds, and his servants flames of fire.' [8] But of the Son he says, 'Your throne, O God, is forever and ever, and the righteous sceptre is the sceptre of your kingdom. [9] You have loved righteousness and hated wickedness; therefore God, your God, has anointed you with the oil of gladness beyond your companions.' [10] And, 'In the beginning, Lord, you founded the earth, and the heavens are the work of your hands; [11] they will perish, but you remain; they will all wear out like clothing; [12] like a cloak you will roll them up, and like clothing they will be changed. But you are the same, and your years will never end.' [13] But to which of the angels has he ever said, 'Sit at my right hand until I make your enemies a footstool for your feet'? [14] Are not all angels spirits in the divine service, sent to serve for the sake of those who are to inherit salvation?

THE OLD AND THE NEW

Hebrews **1:1**

[1]Long ago God spoke to our ancestors in many and various ways by the prophets

THE past is behind us, the future in front. That's the common picture. And yet what we know is our past — it is before us! — and our future is unknown to us. Don't we in fact move backwards as it were towards the future? Don't we look to our past for guidelines as we grope our way into that darkness? Isn't the pilgrimage of faith a bit like that?

God has touched my life in many ways and bit by bit, giving me many bright spells on the way. This is valuable guidance, something to be thankful for. But guidance it is, an invitation to grow. Pining for the honeymoon romance can prevent people from growing in their marriage relationship (so I am told.) It can come of failing to realise that 'the best is yet to be', failing to discern that now is the time for true love to be active 'for better, for worse'.

Hebrews was no doubt written for people who were a bit nostalgic for the past, for the ancestral inheritance. And so they are told here: 'Yes, God has dealt graciously with us for ages past, but now the promises are being corrected in the act of being fulfilled, and the very word EMMANUEL is coming true, truer than all expectation': 'God with us', thanks be to Him.

Why not pause a while in this silence to remember everyone who has awakened me and supported me up to today, and to give thanks for them and pray for blessing on them? Then pray for insight into how God has spoken to me and worked in me through all these contacts, and through his Son, so as to bring me to this day, this new opportunity.

HEIR OF ALL THINGS

Hebrews **1:1-4**

[1] Long ago God spoke to our ancestors in many and various ways by the prophets, [2] but in these last days he has spoken to us by a Son, whom he appointed heir of all things, through whom he also created the worlds. [3] He is the reflection of God's glory and the exact imprint of God's very being, and he sustains all things by his powerful word. When he had made purification for sins, he sat down at the right hand of the Majesty on high, [4] having become as much superior to angels as the name he has inherited is more excellent than theirs.

OUR attention is drawn to the Son; he is the centre, to him we turn. In him 'the whole creation moves', he too is 'the one whom he appointed heir of all things, through whom he also created the worlds'.

Lord Jesus, you are the first and the last, the living One; you died, and you are alive for ever. In the beginning, before the world was, you were with your Father, and you will be with us to the end of the world. In you dwells the whole fullness of God. In you the whole of creation is to be brought together in unity in the plan of fulfilment of the ages, bringing together all things in heaven and on earth.

To you all flesh shall come. To you all shall bring their confession of sin. In you are centred the hopes of all ages, in you the desires of all ages find their correction and fulfilment that will turn out better than all dreams.

I turn to you with my fears and desires, admitting my sin. So often have I seen you in need and failed to offer help to you. So often have I misused the opportunity and the gift you have given me so lavishly.

Gentle Lord, though you have searched me and known me long before I knew it, though you know me so well, I know you love me in spite of all. Thank you for your patience, for your mercy, your grace. Let me realise more and more how great you are. Kindle in me the fire of your love.

SPEAKING

Hebrews **1:1-2**

[1] Long ago God spoke to our ancestors in many and various ways by the prophets, [2] but in these last days he has spoken to us by a Son, whom he appointed heir of all things, through whom he also created the worlds.

GREAT music rises out of silence, without completely filling the silence. So it is with the word of God. He speaks 'in many and various ways', and his silence too is a speaking, behind all other speech. Already in creation he offers himself for us to know, to discern 'his eternal power and divine nature', without saying anything yet. 'The heavens are telling the glory of God', without speech, without words, 'yet their voice goes out through all the earth.' 'There is one teacher', says Ignatius of Antioch, 'who spoke, and it came to be, and what he did in silence is worthy of the Father.'

Yes, he spoke of old 'by the prophets', and sent them to present his message, sometimes in story and parable and poetry, and now and then in significant action. But when at last he speaks 'by a Son', he doesn't send the Son to convey a message, or not mainly for that. The Son is indeed a Prophet, but much more than a prophet. The Son himself is the message; Jesus Christ himself is the Good News. Before Jesus spoke, and after he spoke, the Father is already eloquent in the silent presence of the Son. 'The one who has the word of Jesus', says Ignatius again, 'can listen to his quietness as well, in order to be complete, one with his word and manifest in action'.

Hebrews springs from quiet faith in Jesus Christ, and its aim is to strengthen and deepen faith in him. Let us rest quietly in his company, silently open to the fullness of his love.

THE GREATNESS OF THE SON (1)

Hebrews 1:2-4

[2] but in these last days he has spoken to us by a Son, whom he appointed heir of all things, through whom he also created the worlds. [3] He is the reflection of God's glory and the exact imprint of God's very being, and he sustains all things by his powerful word. When he had made purification for sins, he sat down at the right hand of the Majesty on high, [4] having become as much superior to angels as the name he has inherited is more excellent than theirs.

WHAT a writer often does is create an experience, putting words together in a way that makes notional things real and gives shape to what was nebulous. That is not quite what we have here in *Hebrews*. God is already present on this side of every expression. And before anything is said about the Son, he is already fully himself, fully present to the author and his hearers, and to us too; every expression falls short of conveying the majesty of the One given to us, who has us.

Even so, the author of *Hebrews* has the skill to tell of the Son. Already in this beginning he presents the heart of what he has to say. 'By a Son'. What sort of son? One 'whom he appointed heir of all things' (compare the parable of the vineyard, Matthew 21:37-38). One who was engaged in the creation, who fully represents God, who is the Saviour. Then the author develops these themes, as it were, in a symphony. The central theme is the communion within the fullness of God that is given us in Christ. To express that as far as may be, he draws on the 'many and various ways' of his Jewish heritage. They are the patterns of expression that are

7

available to him and his audience, but Jesus gives them new significance: 'The Scriptures testify to me' (John 5:39). And so we search for Jesus in them. Let us ask him to open them for us (Luke 24:27-32).

For now, we see in a mirror, dimly, but then we will see face to face. Now I know only in part; then I will know fully, even as I have been fully known.

THE GREATNESS OF THE SON (2)

Hebrews 1:3

[3] He is the reflection of God's glory and the exact imprint of God's very being, and he sustains all things by his powerful word. When he had made purification for sins, he sat down at the right hand of the Majesty on high

SAYING 'He is the reflection of God's glory' echoes the praise of wisdom in *The Wisdom of Solomon* (7:25-26), as does saying that he is 'the exact imprint of God's very being'. There is also an echo of the beginning: 'let us make humankind in our image, according to our likeness' (Genesis 1:26-27; compare Wisdom 2:23, and 1 Corinthians 11:7). Not only an echo, but also a promise.

In the man Jesus 'the whole fullness of deity dwells bodily' (Colossians 2:9), to bring us to clothe ourselves with the new self, which is being renewed in knowledge according to the image of its creator (Colossians 3:10), 'until all of us come to the unity of the faith and of the knowledge of the Son of God, to maturity, to the measure of the full stature of Christ' (Ephesians 4:13).

In the man Jesus, 'the image of God' (2 Corinthians 4:4) creation is marvellously fulfilled and restored; he is 'the exact imprint of God's very being' – 'whoever has seen me has seen the Father (John 14:9). As was said already, Jesus is the heir of all the promises.

Along with that we are reminded that Jesus is the one 'through whom he also created the worlds'. He is the one, the same one, but that is so not by virtue of his human nature. It is not as man that Jesus 'sustains all things by his powerful word'. It is not of him as man that it is said that 'all things have been created through him and for him'. Nor is it in virtue of his full humanity that 'he himself is before all things, and in him all things hold together'. And yet in the man Jesus 'all the fullness of God was pleased to dwell, and through him' – yes, through his humanity – 'God was pleased to reconcile to himself all things... by making peace through the blood of his cross' (Colossians 1:17-20).

The Word from heaven, kin to us —
The great little one, weak but strong —
The giver and support of being, and ruler of all that is ...

THE GREATNESS OF THE SON (3)

Hebrews **1:3**

[3] He is the reflection of God's glory and the exact imprint of God's very being, and he sustains all things by his powerful word. When he had made purification for sins, he sat down at the right hand of the Majesty on high

JESUS Christ is the full and final self-communication of the Father, but human thought and discourse about him is never total. Faith in Jesus is simple, but 'many and various ways' are needed to express it even in part (John 21:25).

So Jesus is 'the reflection of God's glory' and 'the exact imprint of God's very being'; he it is who 'sustains all things by his powerful word', and who 'when he had made purification for sins' (of which we shall hear more presently) 'sat down at the right hand of the Majesty on high'.

As he has always been equal to the Father in Godhead, he is Lord in his humanity also, after the Cross, Resurrection and Ascension (Philippians 2:11; compare Romans 10:9). Here something similar is suggested, by saying that Jesus, after his sacrifice, is seated on his royal throne. But here another contrast is used to express his greatness: not that he has received 'the name which is above every name', but, all the same, that he has become 'as much superior to angels as the name he has inherited is more excellent than theirs'.

HIGHER THAN THE ANGELS (1)

Hebrews 1:4

[4] having become as much superior to angels as the name he has inherited is more excellent than theirs.

AS we consider the titles of the Son, we begin to realise how much higher than the angels he is said to be. He excels them as their Creator (compare Colossians 1:15-16); He excels in every way beyond comparison.

Contrasting Jesus with the prophets of old was not meant to disparage the message given through them; the point was to celebrate his greatness rather than to diminish them. The same is true of contrasting Jesus with the angels, those high creatures who surround the throne of the Lord to wait on him (for example in Isaiah 6:1-8). The Son sits on the right hand of the throne, higher yet than their height; exactly because he stooped to be a servant, his humanity too is raised to be Lord.

Jesus did all this for us, to raise us to himself (compare John 14:2-3). Let us ask him to lighten the eyes of our mind to learn how rich is the inheritance that is given us in him and through him, and how great is the power that 'raised him from the dead and seated him at his right hand in the heavenly places, far above all rule and authority and power and dominion, and above every name that is named, not only in this age but also in the age to come' (compare Ephesians 1:18-21).

Oh! To have faith to gaze with the angels on the mystery, to see the order of salvation.

HIGHER THAN THE ANGELS (2)

Hebrews 1:5-9

⁵ For to which of the angels did God ever say, 'You are my Son; today I have begotten you'? Or again, 'I will be his Father, and he will be my Son'? ⁶ And again, when he brings the firstborn into the world, he says, 'Let all God's angels worship him.' ⁷ Of the angels he says, 'He makes his angels winds, and his servants flames of fire.' ⁸ But of the Son he says, 'Your throne, O God, is forever and ever, and the righteous sceptre is the sceptre of your kingdom. ⁹ You have loved righteousness and hated wickedness; therefore God, your God, has anointed you with the oil of gladness beyond your companions.'

IN the first place, the supreme excellence of Jesus is conveyed by the name that has been given him; indeed both quotations come from the context of enthroning the king of Israel: 'You are my son; today I have begotten you' (Psalm 2:7). And again: 'I will be a father to him, and he shall be a son to me' (2 Samuel 7:14). But applied to Jesus they acquire a far finer significance. This is to declare that he is Son, after the cross and resurrection (compare Romans 1:3-4). The old kingship was a shadow compared to the kingship of Jesus Christ. And again we notice that the new thing is conveyed by means of the old expressions. They are employed not to prove the point, but to express it as well as possible.

So, as the *Hebrews*-author continues, he picks up quotations here and there to be used to tell how Jesus Christ excels them all: 'Let all God's angels worship him'. In the original context (the Greek of Deuteronomy 32:43), worshipping God is what is meant, but here God is presented saying this of Jesus, as 'he brings' him, his 'firstborn into the world' (this is open to referring to his first coming into the world, to his coming again in glory, or to his daily coming to us).

The angels are ministers; not so the Son. Once again the words used were addressed to a king, but here they have far far greater significance. He is the Anointed, the Messiah, and more: 'Your throne, O God, is for ever and ever'. Thanks be to him for raising us to share his inheritance (Revelation 1:6; Matthew 25:34; 1 John 2:20; 2 Corinthians 1:21; Romans 8:17; 2 Timothy 2:12).

HIGHER THAN THE ANGELS (3)

Hebrews **1:10-12**

[10] And, 'In the beginning, Lord, you founded the earth, and the heavens are the work of your hands; [11] they will perish, but you remain; they will all wear out like clothing; [12] like a cloak you will roll them up, and like clothing they will be changed. But you are the same, and your years will never end.'

JUST as the words of the Lord in Isaiah 45:23 – 'to me every knee shall bow' – are applied to Jesus in Philippians 2:11, so here the Son is taken to be addressed by the Father in the words of Psalm 102:25-27: 'of the Son he says… "In the beginning, Lord, you founded the earth, and the heavens are the work of your hands; they will perish, but you remain; they will all wear out like clothing; like a cloak you will roll them up, and like clothing they will be changed. But you are the same, and your years will never end".' This is shocking at first sight, and yet it is no more than a development of what has already been said: Jesus is more than a prophet, more than a king, more than an angel, the shining of the glory, the image and likeness, the exact imprint of the very being of the Lord, the living God.

This develops a better notion of the excellence of the Son, indeed it does; but it also deepens the revelation of the Lord God of the covenant, the God who reveals himself to his people. In the Son God reveals himself more fully still; and the Son's being what he is reveals yet more about the life of the living God. How is it revealed that God is love? (compare 1 John 4:7-12).

Here there is room for us to open ourselves to the greatness of the Son, not in order to unfold ideas, but to adore him more loyally, and to come through him to adore the Father in spirit and in truth. Yes, and to do that with the confidence that his Spirit will guide us in the whole truth.

Letter to the Hebrews

Chapter 2

[1] Therefore we must pay greater attention to what we have heard, so that we do not drift away from it. [2] For if the message declared through angels was valid, and every transgression or disobedience received a just penalty, [3] how can we escape if we neglect so great a salvation? It was declared at first through the Lord, and it was attested to us by those who heard him, [4] while God added his testimony by signs and wonders and various miracles, and by gifts of the Holy Spirit, distributed according to his will. [5] Now God did not subject the coming world, about which we are speaking, to angels. [6] But someone has testified somewhere, 'What are human beings that you are mindful of them, or mortals, that you care for them? [7] You have made them for a little while lower than the angels; you have crowned them with glory and honour, [8] subjecting all things under their feet.' Now in subjecting all things to them, God left nothing outside their control. As it is, we do not yet see everything in subjection to them, [9] but we do see Jesus, who for a little while was made lower than the angels, now crowned with glory and honour because of the suffering of death, so that by the grace of God he might taste death for everyone. [10] It was fitting that God, for whom and through whom all things exist, in bringing many children to glory, should make the pioneer of their salvation perfect through sufferings. [11] For the one who sanctifies and those who are sanctified all have one Father. For this reason Jesus is not ashamed to call them brothers and sisters, [12] saying, 'I will proclaim your name to my brothers and sisters, in the midst of the congregation I will praise you.' [13] And again, 'I will put my trust in him.' And again, 'Here am I and the children whom God has given

me.' [14] Since, therefore, the children share flesh and blood, he himself likewise shared the same things, so that through death he might destroy the one who has the power of death, that is, the devil, [15] and free those who all their lives were held in slavery by the fear of death. [16] For it is clear that he did not come to help angels, but the descendants of Abraham. [17] Therefore he had to become like his brothers and sisters in every respect, so that he might be a merciful and faithful high priest in the service of God, to make a sacrifice of atonement for the sins of the people. [18] Because he himself was tested by what he suffered, he is able to help those who are being tested.

SO GREAT A SALVATION

Hebrews **1:13 - 2:4**

[13] But to which of the angels has he ever said, 'Sit at my right hand until I make your enemies a footstool for your feet'? [14] Are not all angels spirits in the divine service, sent to serve for the sake of those who are to inherit salvation? [Chapter 2] [1] Therefore we must pay greater attention to what we have heard, so that we do not drift away from it. [2] For if the message declared through angels was valid, and every transgression or disobedience received a just penalty, [3] how can we escape if we neglect so great a salvation? It was declared at first through the Lord, and it was attested to us by those who heard him, [4] while God added his testimony by signs and wonders and various miracles, and by gifts of the Holy Spirit, distributed according to his will.

AGAIN the *Hebrews*-author cites one of the royal Psalms, which recalls the promise to King David (2 Samuel 7:11-16); the Son is told 'sit at my right hand...' something never said to any angel. The angels, for all their high status and function, are all of them 'spirits in the divine service, sent to serve for the sake of those who are to inherit salvation'.

With this mention of salvation the lesson comes home to us (to the second generation of disciples, and to us in our turn today). To us this most excellent inheritance has been passed on, with all the more pressing a challenge because the manifestation of God's love in it is now full and final. We are not asked for less attention than was asked of those of old. Living true to the spirit of the Gospel is not easier than keeping the letter of the Law, although it is not a matter of keeping law. Jesus said, 'Do not think that I have come to abolish the law or the prophets; I have come not to abolish but to fulfil' (Matthew 5:17). We know what fulfilment he has in mind: ' "Love the Lord with all your heart, and with all your soul, and with all your mind"... "Love your neighbour as yourself". On these two commandments hang all the law and the prophets.' (Matthew 22:37-40; compare 25:31-46; Romans 13:8-10).

Backsliding from the 'law' of love given in and by Jesus the Son of God is not threatened with a punishment from without, but with a terrible loss within (compare John 6:68-69).

Let me not separate myself from you.

THE LEADER OF SALVATION (1)

Hebrews **2:5-12**

[5] Now God did not subject the coming world, about which we are speaking, to angels. [6] But someone has testified somewhere, 'What are human beings that you are mindful of them, or mortals, that you care for them? [7] You have made them for a little while lower than the angels; you have crowned them with glory and honour, [8] subjecting all things under their feet.' Now in subjecting all things to them, God left nothing outside their control. As it is, we do not yet see everything in subjection to them, [9] but we do see Jesus, who for a little while was made lower than the angels, now

crowned with glory and honour because of the suffering of death, so that by the grace of God he might taste death for everyone. [10] It was fitting that God, for whom and through whom all things exist, in bringing many children to glory, should make the pioneer of their salvation perfect through sufferings. [11] For the one who sanctifies and those who are sanctified all have one Father. For this reason Jesus is not ashamed to call them brothers and sisters, [12] saying, 'I will proclaim your name to my brothers and sisters, in the midst of the congregation I will praise you.'

JESUS has come into his own, although we have not yet seen 'all things subjected to him' (1 Corinthians 15:24-28). Yes; God's rule, God's kingdom is established. Yet there is still reason to pray 'thy kingdom come'; has God's grace had its way fully in us, let alone in the world around us? And remember Pascal's remark, that the agony of Jesus will not come to end finally before the end of the world (compare Colossians 1:24). Wherever his people suffer, there he will be with them.

We are invited to wonder at the way God 'for whom and through whom all things exist' manifests his love and his sympathy. Granted that God, as God, is beyond the reach of finite feelings, he is not out of sympathy with them. He shows that in his Son, who, in his humanity, was to 'be made perfect through sufferings' so as to bring 'many children to glory' – 'here am I and the children God has given me'.

'The children share flesh and blood': we were kin with Jesus already before he became one of us, because as he is eternally in God's love so we are creatures of God's love. Once he has come to share our life and suffer for us and with us, he has come yet closer to us to make us holy, to enable us to share his divine life (compare John 17:19). He experienced the human condition at its worst, and could take the anguish on himself (Psalm 22:1-21; compare Matthew 27:46), winning the right to the victory expressed in the same Psalm (22:22).

Oh God, comfort of the afflicted and support of the heavy--burdened, hear the prayers of everyone who calls on you from the heart of any trouble, and grant them in their difficulties the taste of your consolation. We ask this through Christ our Lord.

THE LEADER OF SALVATION (2)

Hebrews 2:13-18

[13] And again, 'I will put my trust in him.' And again, 'Here am I and the children whom God has given me.' [14] Since, therefore, the children share flesh and blood, he himself likewise shared the same things, so that through death he might destroy the one who has the power of death, that is, the devil, [15] and free those who all their lives were held in slavery by the fear of death. [16] For it is clear that he did not come to help angels, but the descendants of Abraham. [17] Therefore he had to become like his brothers and sisters in every respect, so that he might be a merciful and faithful high priest in the service of God, to make a sacrifice of atonement for the sins of the people. [18] Because he himself was tested by what he suffered, he is able to help those who are being tested.

PUT in the mouth of Jesus, the words of Isaiah (8:17-18) – 'Here am I and the children whom God has given me' – accept us as made one with him in 'flesh and blood', and present us to his Father in virtue of his having overcome death by dying.

Now, since Jesus' care is for the descendants of Abraham (compare Isaiah 41:8), 'he had to become like his brothers and sisters in every respect, so that he might be a merciful and faithful high priest in the service of God, to make a sacrifice of atonement for the sins of the people. Because he himself was tested by what he suffered, he is able to help those who are being tested'. The author of *Hebrews* uses these words to make the same point, but with new effect: yes, Jesus is indeed doing what a high priest was meant to do. The name of the old office is used, but with enhanced effect.

Jesus was not born to a priestly line; he is never said to have claimed directly that he was a priest. There was no trace of Temple ritual in the sacrifice on Calvary hill, 'a sack of bones nailed on a pole like a scarecrow, outside the town'. There was, for all that, a prophetic suggestion (Isaiah 53:10), and Jesus' own words (1 Corinthians 11:25), that give ground to discern that his death was more truly a sacrifice than any other (compare Romans 3:25; Ephesians 5:2; 1 Peter 1:19). If he offered himself, then he was a priest indeed, more truly a priest than any other. The central image in *Hebrews* is the Temple and its high priest, an image given new significance in Christ. Here, so far, the image only begins to be presented: Jesus had to become fully like us; he knows what it is to be tempted, to be tried, and he knows what it is to come through victoriously. We can trust him.

Letter to the Hebrews

Chapter 3

[1] Therefore, brothers and sisters, holy partners in a heavenly calling, consider that Jesus, the apostle and high priest of our confession, [2] was faithful to the one who appointed him, just as Moses also 'was faithful in all God's house.' [3] Yet Jesus is worthy of more glory than Moses, just as the builder of a house has more honour than the house itself. [4] (For every house is built by someone, but the builder of all things is God.) [5] Now Moses was faithful in all God's house as a servant, to testify to the things that would be spoken later. [6] Christ, however, was faithful over God's house as a son, and we are his house if we hold firm the confidence and the pride that belong to hope. [7] Therefore, as the Holy Spirit says, 'Today, if you hear his voice, [8] do not harden your hearts as in the rebellion, as on the day of testing in the wilderness, [9] where your ancestors put me to the test, though they had seen my works [10] for forty years. Therefore I was angry with that generation, and I said, "They always go astray in their hearts, and they have not known my ways." [11] As in my anger I swore, "They will not enter my rest." ' [12] Take care, brothers and sisters, that none of you may have an evil, unbelieving heart that turns away from the living God. [13] But exhort one another every day, as long as it is called 'today,' so that none of you may be hardened by the deceitfulness of sin. [14] For we have become partners of Christ, if only we hold our first confidence firm to the end. [15] As it is said, 'Today, if you hear his voice, do not harden your hearts as in the rebellion.' [16] Now who were they who heard and yet were rebellious? Was it not all those who left Egypt under the leadership of Moses? [17] But with whom was he angry forty years? Was it not those who sinned, whose

bodies fell in the wilderness? [18] And to whom did he swear that they would not enter his rest, if not to those who were disobedient? [19] So we see that they were unable to enter because of unbelief.

APOSTLE AND HIGH PRIEST

Hebrews 3:1-6

[1] Therefore, brothers and sisters, holy partners in a heavenly calling, consider that Jesus, the apostle and high priest of our confession, [2] was faithful to the one who appointed him, just as Moses also 'was faithful in all God's house.' [3] Yet Jesus is worthy of more glory than Moses, just as the builder of a house has more honour than the house itself. [4] (For every house is built by someone, but the builder of all things is God.) [5] Now Moses was faithful in all God's house as a servant, to testify to the things that would be spoken later. [6] Christ, however, was faithful over God's house as a son, and we are his house if we hold firm the confidence and the pride that belong to hope.

WE are called 'holy' because we are members of a holy people, called together by God to grow nearer to God. The call comes through Jesus, the Father's messenger, and we are to respond to it through him, with him, and in him. He, then, is the 'apostle and high priest' of our faith and belief. He is to be the centre of our attention and our life.

'All God's house' in which Moses was a faithful servant, testifying to all the Lord's promises, was Israel, the people of God. Jesus in his turn has been a faithful servant to the one who appointed him, and more than a servant, because he is the son of the house, set over it by the builder of the house (yes, and 'builder of all things').

Moses is brought in by the *Hebrews*-author to show something more of the greatness of Jesus. Moses was praised above the prophets: to them the Lord makes himself known

21

in visions and dreams, but with Moses 'I speak face to face… and he beholds the form of the Lord' (Numbers 12:6-8). Moses, indeed, was called to serve the whole people of God rather than any one area of their life. Jesus has a task with just as great a scope, and greater yet, because now 'the people of God' is open to including all the peoples of the world.

TODAY! (1)

Hebrews **3:7-11**

[7] Therefore, as the Holy Spirit says, 'Today, if you hear his voice, [8] do not harden your hearts as in the rebellion, as on the day of testing in the wilderness, [9] where your ancestors put me to the test, though they had seen my works [10] for forty years. Therefore I was angry with that generation, and I said, "They always go astray in their hearts, and they have not known my ways." [11] As in my anger I swore, "They will not enter my rest." '

THE hope of the believer is not optimism, not a confidence that things in this world will get better, but a trust in the Lord whatever happens (compare Habakkuk 3:17-19; Daniel 3:18 – 'but if not…'). Being the people of Jesus Christ means that we go forward in faith through the desert, wholly dependent on his strength to support us on the journey.

Israel's failure in the desert was that they challenged the Lord by asking 'Is the Lord among us or not?' (Exodus 17:7). The Psalm suggests that they showed the same lack of faith throughout the forty years. Just as their present and pressing thirst ousted any memory of the great deeds accomplished for them, so also they couldn't believe that the Lord could settle them in the Promised Land. That was a hardening of the heart, a closing of the mind by people astray (in the worst desert by far, a wilderness of heart), 'people who will not accept my ways'.

Of old, when the fire was kept alive from day to day and covered by night, it had to be rekindled and fuelled every day. Faith is like a fire on the heart's hearth, with all the more need for attention and active fuelling as its object is unseen. Without fuelling we find that it cools to extinction in the face of the more obvious circumstances of the world about us.

'Today, if you hear his voice' – the voice of Jesus now – 'do not harden your hearts as on the day of testing in the wilderness'. Let us pray that he will open our hearts today to the fullness of his love.

TODAY! (2)

Hebrews **3:12-19**

[12] Take care, brothers and sisters, that none of you may have an evil, unbelieving heart that turns away from the living God. [13] But exhort one another every day, as long as it is called 'today,' so that none of you may be hardened by the deceitfulness of sin. [14] For we have become partners of Christ, if only we hold our first confidence firm to the end. [15] As it is said, 'Today, if you hear his voice, do not harden your hearts as in the rebellion.' [16] Now who were they who heard and yet were rebellious? Was it not all those who left Egypt under the leadership of Moses? [17] But with whom was he angry forty years? Was it not those who sinned, whose bodies fell in the wilderness? [18] And to whom did he swear that they would not enter his rest, if not to those who were disobedient? [19] So we see that they were unable to enter because of unbelief.

'MY God, my God, why have you forsaken me?' That is not the cry of 'an evil unbelieving heart', not the shriek of one who 'turns away from the living God'. It is the very

23

opposite, as the end of the Psalm suggests (22:22-31), and as is plain when we notice that the cry, from the depth of darkness, is still a cry to 'my God'. There is a big difference between complaining *to* God about our afflictions and complaining *about* God on account of our afflictions. One springs from faith, the other tends to undermine it. One brings us nearer to Jesus and his Father, the other turns us away from them. The grace of one admits to 'his rest', the danger of the unbelieving other is that it risks being 'unable to enter'.

We are not people 'who left Egypt under the leadership of Moses'; no, 'we have become partners of Christ'. We can be sharers in the life of the Messiah, the Anointed (just as he has shared our life: Hebrews 2:14), 'if only we hold our first confidence firm to the end', not allowing any obstacle to come between us and him 'today'. As 'partners of Christ' we are not alone in this. Jesus is with us and for us, and we are to encourage each other while that 'today' is still to be had.

Lord, almighty God, as you have brought us to the beginning of this day, we pray you to support us with your power: do not allow us to stray into sinful ways, but rather guide us to carry our your righteousness in thought, word and deed. We ask this in the name of Christ our Lord.

Letter to the Hebrews

Chapter 4

[1] Therefore, while the promise of entering his rest is still open, let us take care that none of you should seem to have failed to reach it. [2] For indeed the good news came to us just as to them; but the message they heard did not benefit them, because they were not united by faith with those who listened. [3] For we who have believed enter that rest, just as God has said, 'As in my anger I swore, "They shall not enter my rest," ' though his works were finished at the foundation of the world. [4] For in one place it speaks about the seventh day as follows, 'And God rested on the seventh day from all his works.' [5] And again in this place it says, 'They shall not enter my rest.' [6] Since therefore it remains open for some to enter it, and those who formerly received the good news failed to enter because of disobedience, [7] again he sets a certain day – 'today' – saying through David much later, in the words already quoted, 'Today, if you hear his voice, do not harden your hearts.' [8] For if Joshua had given them rest, God would not speak later about another day. [9] So then, a sabbath rest still remains for the people of God; [10] for those who enter God's rest also cease from their labours as God did from his. [11] Let us therefore make every effort to enter that rest, so that no one may fall through such disobedience as theirs. [12] Indeed, the word of God is living and active, sharper than any two-edged sword, piercing until it divides soul from spirit, joints from marrow; it is able to judge the thoughts and intentions of the heart. [13] And before him no creature is hidden, but all are naked and laid bare to the eyes of the one to whom we must render an account. [14] Since, then, we have a great high priest who has passed through the heavens, Jesus, the Son of God, let us hold fast to our confession. [15] For

we do not have a high priest who is unable to sympathize with our weaknesses, but we have one who in every respect has been tested as we are, yet without sin. [16]Let us therefore approach the throne of grace with boldness, so that we may receive mercy and find grace to help in time of need.

A REST FOR GOD'S PEOPLE

Hebrews 4:1-11

[1] Therefore, while the promise of entering his rest is still open, let us take care that none of you should seem to have failed to reach it. [2]For indeed the good news came to us just as to them; but the message they heard did not benefit them, because they were not united by faith with those who listened. [3]For we who have believed enter that rest, just as God has said, 'As in my anger I swore, "They shall not enter my rest," ' though his works were finished at the foundation of the world. [4]For in one place it speaks about the seventh day as follows, 'And God rested on the seventh day from all his works.' [5]And again in this place it says, 'They shall not enter my rest.' [6]Since therefore it remains open for some to enter it, and those who formerly received the good news failed to enter because of disobedience, [7]again he sets a certain day – 'today' – saying through David much later, in the words already quoted, 'Today, if you hear his voice, do not harden your hearts.' [8]For if Joshua had given them rest, God would not speak later about another day. [9]So then, a sabbath rest still remains for the people of God; [10]for those who enter God's rest also cease from their labours as God did from his. [11]Let us therefore make every effort to enter that rest, so that no one may fall through such disobedience as theirs.

YES; 'in one place it speaks about the seventh day as follows: "And God rested on the seventh day from all his works".' God's rest is ready since the beginning. It was offered in a promise to the people of Israel; the offer did not come to an end when the people entered the promised land, seeing that the Psalm continues to offer it quite a while afterwards. And it is still offered to us; the sun has not yet set on the 'today'. The reasoning in this passage is tricky, but yet again it is the message that counts rather than the argument: 'the promise is still open' and none of you should think you have failed to reach it. The challenge and the opportunity persist, this new 'today'.

Faith is still the entry to the rest, as it was for them of old. But it is not enough to hear the word and accept it. We have accepted a fuller gospel than was given to them, but with the same essential challenge: if we are to benefit from it at all, we must commit ourselves to it in living faith, in word and deed; we must allow it to take hold of us, to unite us with those who truly listen to us, so as to live at one with it, obedient to the Lord who makes himself known in it.

Come, Lord, into the wilderness, as you have been here before; lead me, weakling pilgrim, with your pillars, cloud and fire; hold my spirit, faint from fears from all about me; I walk firmly in your power, but without you feebly fall.

A REST FOR GOD'S PEOPLE (2)

Hebrews **4:11-13**

[11] Let us therefore make every effort to enter that rest, so that no one may fall through such disobedience as theirs. [12] Indeed, the word of God is living and active, sharper than any two-edged sword, piercing until it divides soul from spirit, joints from marrow; it is able to judge the thoughts and intentions of the heart. [13] And before him no creature is hidden, but all are naked and laid bare to the eyes of the one to whom we must render an account.

IT is not enough to belong to the Church; one needs to belong to it internally, from within, alive to the Word of God

27

in spiritual obedience. This means a constant effort (compare, in a similar context, 1 Corinthians 10:12 – 'So if you think you are standing, watch out that you do not fall').

The word of the living God in all its power lives with us and in us, reaches within and without, an awesome warning and a gentle comfort. 'Where can I go from your spirit?' (Psalm 139:7-12); 'Lord, to whom can we go?' (John 6:68); 'In every generation she passes into holy souls and makes them friends of God and prophets' (Wisdom of Solomon 7:27).

The word of God is usually a costly guest for those to whom and through whom it comes, and for everyone who accepts it in faith. It is 'sharper than any two-edged sword, piercing until it divides soul from spirit, joints from marrow', judging 'the thoughts and intentions of the heart'. Knowing each and every one, the word of God offers a unique challenge to each one (compare, for example, Luke 9:57-62; 10:25-42). As it did of old, the word of God still calls people 'in many and various ways', but now it includes a clear call to join in his sacrifice, for each of us to take up our own cross, to be ready to lose our life 'for my sake and for the sake of the gospel' (Mark 8:34-38; compare Hebrews 12:4; 13:13). And yet it is open, two-edged: 'Do you also wish to go away?' (John 6:67).

Search me, O God, and lead me in the way everlasting.

JESUS, THE GREAT HIGH PRIEST (1)

Hebrews **4:14-16**

[14] Since, then, we have a great high priest who has passed through the heavens, Jesus, the Son of God, let us hold fast to our confession. [15] For we do not have a high priest who is unable to sympathize with our weaknesses, but we have one who in every respect has been tested as we are, yet without sin. [16] Let us therefore approach the throne of grace with

boldness, so that we may receive mercy and find grace to help in time of need.

MOSES was not admitted to the earthly Promised Land, for all that he was so high in the Lord's favour, but our great high priest, 'Jesus, the Son of God', 'has passed through the heavens' into the heavenly rest, to the Father. Not that the Father is far away from us, any more than heaven is. We are not separated from him by distance, but by sin, and by our still living this human life. We are to decide how to live, but the grace is God's: 'let us hold fast to our confession', says the *Hebrews*-author, and to Jesus, and that in face of the world.

Lord, never let me in any way separate myself from you.

Great as Jesus is, 'we do not have a high priest who is unable to sympathize with our weakness, but we have one who in every respect has been tested as we are, yet without sin'. Let us then repent, and 'approach the throne of grace, so that we may receive mercy and find grace to help in time of need'.

Soul of the true light, holy Son, make me holy; and let not my soul stray from your land, your company.

'On that day you will ask in my name. I do not say to you that I will ask the Father on your behalf; for the Father himself loves you, because you have loved me, and have believed that I came from God.' (John 16:26-27).

We thank you, Father and Lord, full of joy, because in ascending into heaven your Son raised us also, winning us a place with him in your glory.

29

Letter to the Hebrews

Chapter 5

[1] Every high priest chosen from among mortals is put in charge of things pertaining to God on their behalf, to offer gifts and sacrifices for sins. [2] He is able to deal gently with the ignorant and wayward, since he himself is subject to weakness; [3] and because of this he must offer sacrifice for his own sins as well as for those of the people. [4] And one does not presume to take this honor, but takes it only when called by God, just as Aaron was. [5] So also Christ did not glorify himself in becoming a high priest, but was appointed by the one who said to him, 'You are my Son, today I have begotten you'; [6] as he says also in another place, 'You are a priest forever, according to the order of Melchizedek.' [7] In the days of his flesh, Jesus offered up prayers and supplications, with loud cries and tears, to the one who was able to save him from death, and he was heard because of his reverent submission. [8] Although he was a Son, he learned obedience through what he suffered; [9] and having been made perfect, he became the source of eternal salvation for all who obey him, [10] having been designated by God a high priest according to the order of Melchizedek. [11] About this we have much to say that is hard to explain, since you have become dull in understanding. [12] For though by this time you ought to be teachers, you need someone to teach you again the basic elements of the oracles of God. You need milk, not solid food; [13] for everyone who lives on milk, being still an infant, is unskilled in the word of righteousness. [14] But solid food is for the mature, for those whose faculties have been trained by practice to distinguish good from evil.

JESUS, THE GREAT HIGH PRIEST (2)

Hebrews **5:1-10**

[1] Every high priest chosen from among mortals is put in charge of things pertaining to God on their behalf, to offer gifts and sacrifices for sins. [2] He is able to deal gently with the ignorant and wayward, since he himself is subject to weakness; [3] and because of this he must offer sacrifice for his own sins as well as for those of the people. [4] And one does not presume to take this honor, but takes it only when called by God, just as Aaron was. [5] So also Christ did not glorify himself in becoming a high priest, but was appointed by the one who said to him, 'You are my Son, today I have begotten you'; [6] as he says also in another place, 'You are a priest forever, according to the order of Melchizedek.' [7] In the days of his flesh, Jesus offered up prayers and supplications, with loud cries and tears, to the one who was able to save him from death, and he was heard because of his reverent submission. [8] Although he was a Son, he learned obedience through what he suffered; [9] and having been made perfect, he became the source of eternal salvation for all who obey him, [10] having been designated by God a high priest according to the order of Melchizedek.

JESUS fulfilled the requirements of being a high priest under the old law, and did much more than fulfil them. He was a man, a human being, one of us, standing before God on our behalf. As a man, 'he did not glorify himself… he did not presume to take this honour'; it was God who appointed him 'a priest for ever according to the order of Melchizedek'.

Jesus had learnt what it is to be weak, 'and yet without sin'. He did not have to 'offer sacrifice for his own sins', and yet he offered himself for us sinners: 'for our sake God made him to be sin who knew no sin, so that in him we might become the righteousness of God' (2 Corinthians 5:21; compare Romans 8:3; Galatians 3:13; 1 Corinthians 1:30).

31

Citing 'the days of his flesh', the *Hebrews*-author recalls Jesus' agony in the garden. What we are offered here is no picture of ritual offering, but agony, Jesus praying 'with loud cries and tears', yes, 'Not my will, but yours'. 'He was heard', indeed, but not immediately. 'Although he was Son' (compare 1:3 above and Philippians 2:6-8) Jesus had to learn to be a true man, 'through what he suffered', and to be a true high priest, a true bridge between God and man, himself 'a source of eternal salvation for all who obey him'.

Now I shall begin to be a disciple. (Ignatius of Antioch, facing death in the arena).
If the Son learnt obedience by suffering, are we not called much more to do likewise? (John Chrysostom).

A WARNING NOT TO FALL AWAY

Hebrews 5:11 - 6:2

[11] About this we have much to say that is hard to explain, since you have become dull in understanding. [12] For though by this time you ought to be teachers, you need someone to teach you again the basic elements of the oracles of God. You need milk, not solid food; [13] for everyone who lives on milk, being still an infant, is unskilled in the word of righteousness. [14] But solid food is for the mature, for those whose faculties have been trained by practice to distinguish good from evil. [Chapter 6] [1] Therefore let us go on toward perfection, leaving behind the basic teaching about Christ, and not laying again the foundation: repentance from dead works and faith toward God, [2] instruction about baptisms, laying on of hands, resurrection of the dead, and eternal judgment.

BODILY and personal growth was part of the human history of Jesus until the end, while the 'exact imprint' of the Father's very being, the 'image and likeness' of his love thereby became more and more evident in him. It was not at his coming into the world that he came to his full growth. Why be surprised then that his people don't straight away become adults in the Faith? The aim is to be brought to a full human maturity, the measure of which is the fullness of Christ (Ephesians 4:13-15).

On the way there we can grow cold, and fall away from our first love (Revelation 2:4-5; 3:1-3, 15-22). We tend to grow lazy and reluctant to grow spiritually, and even lose courage, from fear that growing will be too painful. But it won't do to content ourselves with babies' milk. We can't stop in one place. Trying to do that lands us in worse dangers (John 6:68 again). 'Being at our ease in Zion' can prevent us venturing in meditation and prayer into the depth of the great mystery of our religion; it can hinder our opening up to eternal love. Indeed, without risking it, without opening up, we are in danger of withering in dullness, even of losing faith. If we do take the risk of opening up, we will be drawn to a life better than all expectation (John 10:10).

O! To have faith to gaze with angels into the mystery of salvation ... O! My soul, see how fitting is this divine person; venture your life on him and cast on him your burden. He is a man to sympathize with all your weaknesses; he is God to win the throne over devil, flesh, and world.

Letter to the Hebrews

Chapter 6

[1] Therefore let us go on toward perfection, leaving behind the basic teaching about Christ, and not laying again the foundation: repentance from dead works and faith toward God, [2] instruction about baptisms, laying on of hands, resurrection of the dead, and eternal judgment. [3] And we will do this, if God permits. [4] For it is impossible to restore again to repentance those who have once been enlightened, and have tasted the heavenly gift, and have shared in the Holy Spirit, [5] and have tasted the goodness of the word of God and the powers of the age to come, [6] and then have fallen away, since on their own they are crucifying again the Son of God and are holding him up to contempt. [7] Ground that drinks up the rain falling on it repeatedly, and that produces a crop useful to those for whom it is cultivated, receives a blessing from God. [8] But if it produces thorns and thistles, it is worthless and on the verge of being cursed; its end is to be burned over. [9] Even though we speak in this way, beloved, we are confident of better things in your case, things that belong to salvation. [10] For God is not unjust; he will not overlook your work and the love that you showed for his sake in serving the saints, as you still do. [11] And we want each one of you to show the same diligence so as to realize the full assurance of hope to the very end, [12] so that you may not become sluggish, but imitators of those who through faith and patience inherit the promises. [13] When God made a promise to Abraham, because he had no one greater by whom to swear, he swore by himself, [14] saying, 'I will surely bless you and multiply you.' [15] And thus Abraham, having patiently endured, obtained the promise. [16] Human beings, of course, swear by someone greater than themselves, and

an oath given as confirmation puts an end to all dispute. [17] In the same way, when God desired to show even more clearly to the heirs of the promise the unchangeable character of his purpose, he guaranteed it by an oath, [18] so that through two unchangeable things, in which it is impossible that God would prove false, we who have taken refuge might be strongly encouraged to seize the hope set before us. [19] We have this hope, a sure and steadfast anchor of the soul, a hope that enters the inner shrine behind the curtain, [20] where Jesus, a forerunner on our behalf, has entered, having become a high priest forever according to the order of Melchizedek.

DO NOT TURN YOUR BACK ON THE LIGHT

Hebrews 6:1-6

[1] Therefore let us go on toward perfection, leaving behind the basic teaching about Christ, and not laying again the foundation: repentance from dead works and faith toward God, [2] instruction about baptisms, laying on of hands, resurrection of the dead, and eternal judgment. [3] And we will do this, if God permits. [4] For it is impossible to restore again to repentance those who have once been enlightened, and have tasted the heavenly gift, and have shared in the Holy Spirit, [5] and have tasted the goodness of the word of God and the powers of the age to come, [6] and then have fallen away, since on their own they are crucifying again the Son of God and are holding him up to contempt.

'THOSE who have once been enlightened, and have tasted the heavenly gift, and have shared in the Holy Spirit, and have tasted the goodness of the word of God and the powers of the age to come', how could they ever fall away from that? A warning question.

If the Faith has truly taken root in them, it is hard to believe that anyone could turn back from it. If some did so, he says, 'it is impossible to restore them to repentance … since for their own part they are crucifying again the Son of God and are holding him up to contempt'. 'Impossible' is a hard word, is it not, even for those who knew what they were doing (compare Luke 23:34; Acts 7:60; 1 Corinthians 2:8).

We all know of people who have apparently turned their backs on the Faith they were brought up in, or to which they were converted. But surely it is unlikely that this terrible description of backsliding can be applied to many of them, if indeed to any at all. Perhaps it is best that we take it as a warning to ourselves! It is not our place to judge where anyone is in the sight of God, or to set limits to God's mercy. Anyhow, is it not possible that the original hold that the Faith had on some people was missing somehow? Could it be that their departure was due to misunderstanding or unfortunate experience, honestly reacted to? If there is to be blame, could it perhaps fall rather on others? (Mark 9:42!).

It can never be wrong to resist God if it is done out of genuine care for the truth. Christ will approve of someone's preferring the truth to him, because before he is Christ, he is the truth. If one turns from him towards the truth, one will not go far along that road without landing in his arms. (Simone Weil)

DON'T BE LAZY!

Hebrews 6:7-12

[7] Ground that drinks up the rain falling on it repeatedly, and that produces a crop useful to those for whom it is cultivated, receives a blessing from God. [8] But if it produces thorns and thistles, it is worthless and on the verge of being cursed; its end is to be burned over. [9] Even though we speak in this way, beloved, we are confident of better things in your case, things that belong to salvation. [10] For God is not

unjust; he will not overlook your work and the love that you showed for his sake in serving the saints, as you still do. [11] And we want each one of you to show the same diligence so as to realize the full assurance of hope to the very end, [12] so that you may not become sluggish, but imitators of those who through faith and patience inherit the promises.

THE parable of the ground is a hard warning too, but it has two sides to it (compare Matthew 7:16; 13:3-8, 19-23). The *Hebrews*-author mentions the sharp side, for sure, but does not see that as appropriate to his dear friends, his 'beloved'. God will not overlook the way their faith has been proved 'in serving the saints, as you still do' out of love for them as his people. So the author urges them to be just as diligent in nourishing every aspect of their faith, so as to 'realize the full assurance of hope to the very end'.

If he talks severely to his audience, it is to wake them up rather than to condemn them, acknowledging the good they do and encouraging them to discern more fully 'the riches of his grace that he lavished on us' in Jesus Christ (compare Ephesians 1:3-14).

It is difficult for one to know where one has reached in the spiritual pilgrimage. I am not the one to judge how active my faith is, how pure my motives, and even how right is my notion of God, of Jesus Christ, of 'the great mystery of our religion' (1 Timothy 3:16). But 'I know the one in whom I have put my trust' (2 Timothy 1:12), and what I can do practically is follow the light given me, doing what is to hand, and staying open to greater challenges to come (compare Matthew 19:16-22). Spiritually I can aim my worship in faith and hope beyond every partial notion and idea into the heart of the love that fulfils and supports it all.

GOD'S SURE PROMISE

Hebrews **6:13-20**

[13] When God made a promise to Abraham, because he had no one greater by whom to swear, he swore by himself, [14] saying, 'I will surely bless you and multiply you.' [15] And thus Abraham, having patiently endured, obtained the promise. [16] Human beings, of course, swear by someone greater than themselves, and an oath given as confirmation puts an end to all dispute. [17] In the same way, when God desired to show even more clearly to the heirs of the promise the unchangeable character of his purpose, he guaranteed it by an oath, [18] so that through two unchangeable things, in which it is impossible that God would prove false, we who have taken refuge might be strongly encouraged to seize the hope set before us. [19] We have this hope, a sure and steadfast anchor of the soul, a hope that enters the inner shrine behind the curtain, [20] where Jesus, a forerunner on our behalf, has entered, having become a high priest forever according to the order of Melchizedek.

'FAITH and patience' are to be characteristic of God's people, from Abraham right up to today. It is enough for them that God has given his word, expressing an unchangeable resolve. Enough to encourage us to 'seize the hope set before us'; the hope that was offered to Abraham and fulfilled for him in a way, but fulfilled yet more wonderfully for us. The new hope offered to us, as a sure and steadfast anchor for our life, goes through 'to the inner shrine behind the curtain, where Jesus has entered, a forerunner on our behalf, having become a high priest for ever according to the order of Melchizedek'.

Here we are deftly brought back to the picture of the Temple and its rites, and to the way that Jesus fulfils and transposes it all. Our hope goes through into the holy of holies, into the presence of the Father, with Jesus who has gone through on our behalf (compare 4:15); he is our hope.

Through him, and with him, and in him, we are there already. He is not a temporary high priest; he is there for ever on our behalf (compare 7:23-25 below). Jesus does not stand in the order of Aaron or the Levites, but in the higher order of Melchizedek, king and priest, fulfilling and completing the significance of that too.

O! Infinite strength of the love, the overpowering grace; the unchanging promise lasting ever more. This my anchor on the deep, that God's mind will never change. – He has gone before me through the deep, through fire and water into that blessed land; there he intercedes before the throne, forgiving freely all my faults.

39

Letter to the Hebrews

Chapter 7

[1] This 'King Melchizedek of Salem, priest of the Most High God, met Abraham as he was returning from defeating the kings and blessed him'; [2] and to him Abraham apportioned 'one-tenth of everything.' His name, in the first place, means 'king of righteousness'; next he is also king of Salem, that is, 'king of peace.' [3] Without father, without mother, without genealogy, having neither beginning of days nor end of life, but resembling the Son of God, he remains a priest forever. [4] See how great he is! Even Abraham the patriarch gave him a tenth of the spoils. [5] And those descendants of Levi who receive the priestly office have a commandment in the law to collect tithes from the people, that is, from their kindred, though these also are descended from Abraham. [6] But this man, who does not belong to their ancestry, collected tithes from Abraham and blessed him who had received the promises. [7] It is beyond dispute that the inferior is blessed by the superior. [8] In the one case, tithes are received by those who are mortal; in the other, by one of whom it is testified that he lives. [9] One might even say that Levi himself, who receives tithes, paid tithes through Abraham, [10] for he was still in the loins of his ancestor when Melchizedek met him. [11] Now if perfection had been attainable through the levitical priesthood – for the people received the law under this priesthood – what further need would there have been to speak of another priest arising according to the order of Melchizedek, rather than one according to the order of Aaron? [12] For when there is a change in the priesthood, there is necessarily a change in the law as well. [13] Now the one of whom these things are spoken belonged to another tribe, from which no one has ever served

at the altar. [14] For it is evident that our Lord was descended from Judah, and in connection with that tribe Moses said nothing about priests. [15] It is even more obvious when another priest arises, resembling Melchizedek, [16] one who has become a priest, not through a legal requirement concerning physical descent, but through the power of an indestructible life. [17] For it is attested of him, 'You are a priest forever, according to the order of Melchizedek.' [18] There is, on the one hand, the abrogation of an earlier commandment because it was weak and ineffectual [19] (for the law made nothing perfect); there is, on the other hand, the introduction of a better hope, through which we approach God. [20] This was confirmed with an oath; for others who became priests took their office without an oath, [21] but this one became a priest with an oath, because of the one who said to him, 'The Lord has sworn and will not change his mind, "You are a priest forever" ' – [22] accordingly Jesus has also become the guarantee of a better covenant. [23] Furthermore, the former priests were many in number, because they were prevented by death from continuing in office; [24] but he holds his priesthood permanently, because he continues forever. [25] Consequently he is able for all time to save those who approach God through him, since he always lives to make intercession for them. [26] For it was fitting that we should have such a high priest, holy, blameless, undefiled, separated from sinners, and exalted above the heavens. [27] Unlike the other high priests, he has no need to offer sacrifices day after day, first for his own sins, and then for those of the people; this he did once for all when he offered himself. [28] For the law appoints as high priests those who are subject to weakness, but the word of the oath, which came later than the law, appoints a Son who has been made perfect forever.

MELCHIZEDEK

Hebrews 7:1-10

[1] This 'King Melchizedek of Salem, priest of the Most High God, met Abraham as he was returning from defeating the kings and blessed him'; [2] and to him Abraham apportioned 'one-tenth of everything.' His name, in the first place, means 'king of righteousness'; next he is also king of Salem, that is, 'king of peace.' [3] Without father, without mother, without genealogy, having neither beginning of days nor end of life, but resembling the Son of God, he remains a priest forever. [4] See how great he is! Even Abraham the patriarch gave him a tenth of the spoils. [5] And those descendants of Levi who receive the priestly office have a commandment in the law to collect tithes from the people, that is, from their kindred, though these also are descended from Abraham. [6] But this man, who does not belong to their ancestry, collected tithes from Abraham and blessed him who had received the promises. [7] It is beyond dispute that the inferior is blessed by the superior. [8] In the one case, tithes are received by those who are mortal; in the other, by one of whom it is testified that he lives. [9] One might even say that Levi himself, who receives tithes, paid tithes through Abraham, [10] for he was still in the loins of his ancestor when Melchizedek met him.

THE *Hebrews*-author's intention is not to discuss an historical man, but to meditate on what is said and what is not said in the text quoted (Gen 14:17-20). Melchizedek is called 'king of righteousness' and 'king of peace'. There is no mention of parents or lineage, as though he had 'neither beginning of days nor end of life' – he is presented as a wonder, without previous background or subsequent history. We are not told of his dying and leaving his priesthood to his son, as we are told of Aaron (Numbers 20:22-29). Does that not suggest that Melchizedek's priesthood persists?

Does not this make him resemble 'the Son of God', who 're-mains a priest for ever'?

It was Melchizedek who blessed Abraham 'the patri-arch', 'the father of us all', so that Abraham offered him a tithe. That proves that he is superior not only to Abraham, but to all descendants of Abraham, including especially the priests of the tribe of Levi. They die in their turn, but Melchizedek is 'one of whom it is testified that he lives'.

Before Abraham was, I am. (John 8:48-59).
And I, when I am lifted up from the earth, will draw all people to myself. (John 12:32).
Let us go to the throne of grace by faith, the way is open and free, where Jesus is our high priest on high in the presence of the Father. He is the perfect intercessor, who has made us one with God; all that have breath beneath the sky, give praise to the Son of Man!

THE PRIESTHOOD OF MELCHIZEDEK

Hebrews 7:11-19

[11] Now if perfection had been attainable through the levitical priesthood – for the people received the law under this priesthood – what further need would there have been to speak of another priest arising according to the order of Melchizedek, rather than one according to the order of Aaron? [12] For when there is a change in the priesthood, there is necessarily a change in the law as well. [13] Now the one of whom these things are spoken belonged to another tribe, from which no one has ever served at the altar. [14] For it is ev-ident that our Lord was descended from Judah, and in con-nection with that tribe Moses said nothing about priests. [15] It is even more obvious when another priest arises, resem-bling Melchizedek, [16] one who has become a priest, not through a legal requirement concerning physical descent, but through the power of an indestructible life. [17] For it is

attested of him, 'You are a priest forever, according to the order of Melchizedek.' [18] There is, on the one hand, the abrogation of an earlier commandment because it was weak and ineffectual [19] (for the law made nothing perfect); there is, on the other hand, the introduction of a better hope, through which we approach God.

THE priesthood of the tribe of Levi and the Law were closely connected with each other, and were, both of them, much later than Melchizedek. So did they not have a much fuller relationship with God than was available through Melchizedek? But the Psalm was later yet (compare 4:7-9), and it insists on speaking 'of another priest arising according to the order of Melchizedek rather... than of Aaron'.

'Now the one of whom these things are spoken' does not come from the tribe of Levi. Our Lord Jesus is of the tribe of Judah, a non-priestly tribe according to the Law. 'It is even more obvious' when we recall that this other priest has become priest not by human inheritance but by 'the power of an indestructible life'. He has indeed become 'a priest for ever'. The point of all this is that the old order is now superseded; it has become unprofitable, because now there has been established for us 'a better hope, through which we approach God'.

Of old, when indeed God revealed himself to his people in 'many and various ways', the ways of the old Temple worship were part of that. Only now, when the Gospel has come to fulfil the promise, are the old ways become ineffectual – if they are clung to as though they were enough without the Gospel (compare Matthew 9:16-17). It is quite another thing to find in the old its promise of the new (compare Matthew 13. 52). Is not this true also of God's dealing with those of old who lived before the coming of the Law, including Melchizedek, and those ever since who have not yet heard the Gospel effectively? God's generosity is always greater than even God-given human arrangements.

… as once you accepted the gifts of your servant Abel, the sacrifice of Abraham, our father in faith, and the bread and wine offered by your priest Melchizedek.

THE PRIESTHOOD OF JESUS

Hebrews 7:20-28

[20] This was confirmed with an oath; for others who became priests took their office without an oath, [21] but this one became a priest with an oath, because of the one who said to him, 'The Lord has sworn and will not change his mind, "You are a priest forever" ' – [22] accordingly Jesus has also become the guarantee of a better covenant. [23] Furthermore, the former priests were many in number, because they were prevented by death from continuing in office; [24] but he holds his priesthood permanently, because he continues forever. [25] Consequently he is able for all time to save those who approach God through him, since he always lives to make intercession for them. [26] For it was fitting that we should have such a high priest, holy, blameless, undefiled, separated from sinners, and exalted above the heavens. [27] Unlike the other high priests, he has no need to offer sacrifices day after day, first for his own sins, and then for those of the people; this he did once for all when he offered himself. [28] For the law appoints as high priests those who are subject to weakness, but the word of the oath, which came later than the law, appoints a Son who has been made perfect forever.

FOLLOWING the author of the *Letter to the Hebrews* is like climbing a mountain. We go step by step, sometimes side-stepping, often laboriously, thinking we see the summit in reach and then finding another climb ahead. All the same, we get many a glimpse of the summit that keeps us climbing in hope.

The man Jesus also has come to guarantee a better covenant than the old one, because the Lord has sworn an oath to him, 'and will not change his mind, "You are a priest for ever." ' Death will not prevent him from continuing in office; he has no need of successors, because he is a priest for ever. That is why 'he is able for all time to save those who approach God through him, since he always lives to make intercession for them.'

Is this the high point? Melchizedek has given us a glimpse of the sort of high priest who is fitting for us, but the fulfilment of that glimpse in Jesus is far higher and fuller. In Jesus we have one who is 'holy, blameless, undefiled, separated from sinners, and exalted above the heavens', one who has 'no need to offer sacrifices day after day, first for his own sins, and then for those of the people; this he did once for all when he offered himself.' The high priests of the Law are 'subject to weakness, but the word of the oath, which came later than the Law, appoints a Son who has been made perfect for ever.'

There my Jesus has ascended, and there he intercedes.

Letter to the Hebrews

Chapter 8

[1] Now the main point in what we are saying is this: we have such a high priest, one who is seated at the right hand of the throne of the Majesty in the heavens, [2] a minister in the sanctuary and the true tent that the Lord, and not any mortal, has set up. [3] For every high priest is appointed to offer gifts and sacrifices; hence it is necessary for this priest also to have something to offer. [4] Now if he were on earth, he would not be a priest at all, since there are priests who offer gifts according to the law. [5] They offer worship in a sanctuary that is a sketch and shadow of the heavenly one; for Moses, when he was about to erect the tent, was warned, 'See that you make everything according to the pattern that was shown you on the mountain.' [6] But Jesus has now obtained a more excellent ministry, and to that degree he is the mediator of a better covenant, which has been enacted through better promises. [7] For if that first covenant had been faultless, there would have been no need to look for a second one. [8] God finds fault with them when he says: 'The days are surely coming, says the Lord, when I will establish a new covenant with the house of Israel and with the house of Judah; [9] not like the covenant that I made with their ancestors, on the day when I took them by the hand to lead them out of the land of Egypt; for they did not continue in my covenant, and so I had no concern for them, says the Lord. [10] This is the covenant that I will make with the house of Israel after those days, says the Lord: I will put my laws in their minds, and write them on their hearts, and I will be their God, and they shall be my people. [11] And they shall not teach one another or say to each other, "Know the Lord," for they shall all know me, from the least of them to the greatest. [12] For I will

be merciful toward their iniquities, and I will remember their sins no more.' [13] In speaking of 'a new covenant,' he has made the first one obsolete. And what is obsolete and growing old will soon disappear.

THE PRIEST OF THE NEW COVENANT

Hebrews **8:1-6**

[1] Now the main point in what we are saying is this: we have such a high priest, one who is seated at the right hand of the throne of the Majesty in the heavens, [2] a minister in the sanctuary and the true tent that the Lord, and not any mortal, has set up. [3] For every high priest is appointed to offer gifts and sacrifices; hence it is necessary for this priest also to have something to offer. [4] Now if he were on earth, he would not be a priest at all, since there are priests who offer gifts according to the law. [5] They offer worship in a sanctuary that is a sketch and shadow of the heavenly one; for Moses, when he was about to erect the tent, was warned, 'See that you make everything according to the pattern that was shown you on the mountain.' [6] But Jesus has now obtained a more excellent ministry, and to that degree he is the mediator of a better covenant, which has been enacted through better promises.

THE summit is higher yet. It is not a matter of replacing an earthly priest in an earthly Temple, but of shifting the whole Temple to a higher plane (compare John 4: 21-24). Jesus has 'a more excellent ministry'; he is not only a priest but a king as well, who has taken his seat 'at the right hand of the throne of the Majesty in the heavens, a minister in the sanctuary and the true tent that the Lord, and not any mortal, has set up.'

Looked at from an earthly point of view, Jesus fulfils the pattern of the earthly high priest: he has an offering, and has gone into a sanctuary. The crucial difference is that what he offers in sacrifice is his own human life, and that the sanctuary is heaven. From the point of view of the word of God, the comparison is reversed. The earthly Temple and its rites were 'a sketch and shadow of the heavenly one'. They in their place and time were 'in a glass darkly' a reflection of a heavenly model. The *Hebrews*-author says that God had shown the pattern to Moses on the mountain, but that Jesus Christ, Son of God made man, has taken the significance of that pattern to its fulfilment by his going beyond all pictorial patterns and images 'through the heavens' (4:14), offering himself (7:27), and ascending victorious to 'the right hand of the Majesty', to the heavenly presence of the Father.

There is yet more to be acknowledged: 'Jesus has now obtained a more excellent ministry', as 'mediator of a better covenant' based on 'better promises'. We have still further to climb.

How I love the pilgrims as they climb the steep, on their feet and hands; on my knees I will reach the top.

THE OLD COVENANT MADE OBSOLETE?

Hebrews 8:7-13

[7] For if that first covenant had been faultless, there would have been no need to look for a second one. [8] God finds fault with them when he says: 'The days are surely coming, says the Lord, when I will establish a new covenant with the house of Israel and with the house of Judah; [9] not like the covenant that I made with their ancestors, on the day when I took them by the hand to lead them out of the land of Egypt; for they did not continue in my covenant, and so I had no concern for them, says the Lord. [10] This is the covenant that I will make with the house of Israel after those days, says the Lord: I will put my laws in their minds, and write them on their hearts, and I will be their God, and they shall be my people. [11] And they shall not teach one another

or say to each other, "Know the Lord," for they shall all know me, from the least of them to the greatest. [12] For I will be merciful toward their iniquities, and I will remember their sins no more.' [13] In speaking of 'a new covenant,' he has made the first one obsolete. And what is obsolete and growing old will soon disappear.

'WOULD that all the Lord's people were prophets, and that the Lord would put his spirit on them!' (Compare Numbers 11:25-29). The old covenant was made to foster a closer relationship between the Lord and his people. It did not bring that to fulfilment. It was broken again and again. In this quotation (Jeremiah 31:31-34) God finds fault with his people for their unfaithfulness; and yet, in promising a new covenant that will be fully effective, he acknowledges that the first one did not work, and makes it obsolete.

How will the new covenant be different? 'I will put my laws in their minds, and write them on their hearts'. Even the old Law was not really meant to come merely from outside: 'The word is very near to you; it is in your mouth and in your heart' (compare Deuteronomy 30:11-14; Isaiah 51:7; Romans 2:13-15; Romans 10:4-13); 'And I will be their God, and they shall be my people' (compare 2 Corinthians 6:16; Ezekiel 37:27). In the new covenant the purpose of the old will be fulfilled, 'the hopes and fears of all the years' will be satisfied and healed in the Son, Emmanuel.

This covenant is to be between God and his whole people, newly made whole ('a new covenant with the house of Israel and the house of Judah'), yes; but it is also to be between God and every one of his people: 'They shall all know me, from the least of them to the greatest.' He will no longer hold their sins against them: 'I will be merciful towards their iniquities, and I will remember their sins no more'. He will give beyond all merit, with a giving that invites rather than demands a response (1 John 4:9-10; Romans 5:6-7; Galatians 2:20).

Letter to the Hebrews

Chapter 9

[1] Now even the first covenant had regulations for worship and an earthly sanctuary. [2] For a tent was constructed, the first one, in which were the lampstand, the table, and the bread of the Presence; this is called the Holy Place. [3] Behind the second curtain was a tent called the Holy of Holies. [4] In it stood the golden altar of incense and the ark of the covenant overlaid on all sides with gold, in which there were a golden urn holding the manna, and Aaron's rod that budded, and the tablets of the covenant; [5] above it were the cherubim of glory overshadowing the mercy seat. Of these things we cannot speak now in detail. [6] Such preparations having been made, the priests go continually into the first tent to carry out their ritual duties; [7] but only the high priest goes into the second, and he but once a year, and not without taking the blood that he offers for himself and for the sins committed unintentionally by the people. [8] By this the Holy Spirit indicates that the way into the sanctuary has not yet been disclosed as long as the first tent is still standing. [9] This is a symbol of the present time, during which gifts and sacrifices are offered that cannot perfect the conscience of the worshiper, [10] but deal only with food and drink and various baptisms, regulations for the body imposed until the time comes to set things right. [11] But when Christ came as a high priest of the good things that have come, then through the greater and perfect tent (not made with hands, that is, not of this creation), [12] he entered once for all into the Holy Place, not with the blood of goats and calves, but with his own blood, thus obtaining eternal redemption. [13] For if the blood of goats and bulls, with the sprinkling of the ashes of a heifer, sanctifies those who have been defiled so that their

flesh is purified, [14] how much more will the blood of Christ, who through the eternal Spirit offered himself without blemish to God, purify our conscience from dead works to worship the living God! [15] For this reason he is the mediator of a new covenant, so that those who are called may receive the promised eternal inheritance, because a death has occurred that redeems them from the transgressions under the first covenant. [16] Where a will is involved, the death of the one who made it must be established. [17] For a will takes effect only at death, since it is not in force as long as the one who made it is alive. [18] Hence not even the first covenant was inaugurated without blood. [19] For when every commandment had been told to all the people by Moses in accordance with the law, he took the blood of calves and goats, with water and scarlet wool and hyssop, and sprinkled both the scroll itself and all the people, [20] saying, 'This is the blood of the covenant that God has ordained for you.' [21] And in the same way he sprinkled with the blood both the tent and all the vessels used in worship. [22] Indeed, under the law almost everything is purified with blood, and without the shedding of blood there is no forgiveness of sins. [23] Thus it was necessary for the sketches of the heavenly things to be purified with these rites, but the heavenly things themselves need better sacrifices than these. [24] For Christ did not enter a sanctuary made by human hands, a mere copy of the true one, but he entered into heaven itself, now to appear in the presence of God on our behalf. [25] Nor was it to offer himself again and again, as the high priest enters the Holy Place year after year with blood that is not his own; [26] for then he would have had to suffer again and again since the foundation of the world. But as it is, he has appeared once for all at the end of the age to remove sin by the sacrifice of himself. [27] And just as it is appointed for mortals to die once, and after that the judgment, [28] so Christ, having been offered once to bear the sins of many, will appear a second time, not to deal with sin, but to save those who are eagerly waiting for him.

THE EARTHLY SANCTUARY

Hebrews 9:1-5

[1] Now even the first covenant had regulations for worship and an earthly sanctuary. [2] For a tent was constructed, the first one, in which were the lampstand, the table, and the bread of the Presence; this is called the Holy Place. [3] Behind the second curtain was a tent called the Holy of Holies. [4] In it stood the golden altar of incense and the ark of the covenant overlaid on all sides with gold, in which there were a golden urn holding the manna, and Aaron's rod that budded, and the tablets of the covenant; [5] above it were the cherubim of glory overshadowing the mercy seat. Of these things we cannot speak now in detail.

ONE can sense in this passage a fondness for the past, for the arrangement and instruments of the earthly sanctuary as it was to be (compare Maccabees 1:21-23). All this is expected to be just as familiar to the hearers or readers as to the author of the *Letter*, but still they are allowed a moment to dwell lovingly on a memory of 'the golden altar of incense and the ark of the covenant overlaid on all sides with gold', and within that 'a golden urn holding the manna, and Aaron's rod that budded, and the tablets of the covenant', and above it 'the cherubim of glory overshadowing the mercy-seat'.

However dear these memories, they are not to be clung to any more (no more details!); it will not do to remain in that earthly place. Jesus has opened the way into the heavenly sanctuary, and we must go forward there or lose everything. Letting the old order go is the only way to save the heart of it, to reach the fulfilment it prepared and promised. In a word, they (and we) are faced by the age-old challenge of God's word (compare above 4:12; Genesis 12:1, 22:1-19; Matthew 10:39, 16:25; John 12:24-26; Philippians 3:1-14; and elsewhere).

The challenge would not be a challenge if the old had not been a valuable and dear gift; yes, indeed, and a means of grace too, drawing people nearer to God (1 Kings 8:27-53). 'Ask for the ancient paths', it was said (Jeremiah 6:16); but immediately, ask 'where the good way lies, and walk in it'. To find the good way takes the gift of wisdom; and it takes the gift of faith, hope and charity to walk in it although it seems for now to be against the grain.

CHRIST'S PERFECT SACRIFICE

Hebrews **9:6-12**

[6] Such preparations having been made, the priests go continually into the first tent to carry out their ritual duties; [7] but only the high priest goes into the second, and he but once a year, and not without taking the blood that he offers for himself and for the sins committed unintentionally by the people. [8] By this the Holy Spirit indicates that the way into the sanctuary has not yet been disclosed as long as the first tent is still standing. [9] This is a symbol of the present time, during which gifts and sacrifices are offered that cannot perfect the conscience of the worshiper, [10] but deal only with food and drink and various baptisms, regulations for the body imposed until the time comes to set things right. [11] But when Christ came as a high priest of the good things that have come, then through the greater and perfect tent (not made with hands, that is, not of this creation), [12] he entered once for all into the Holy Place, not with the blood of goats and calves, but with his own blood, thus obtaining eternal redemption.

CONSIDERING the old order, and remembering that it too was established by the Holy Spirit, the author of *Hebrews* sees in it an indication 'that the way into the sanctuary' (into the presence of God) had not 'been disclosed as long as the first tabernacle' stood. Even the high priest had access to the sanctuary, the Holy of Holies, only once a year; and to do that he needed to be ritually purified himself. Plainly this is a symbol, a parable, a foreshadowing of what is to be fulfilled in the new order.

If true and internal forgiveness was available for the sins of the people of old, it came to them too by the grace and merit of the Son (compare 1 Corinthians 10:4, 9; John 1:11-13, 8:56). What is said here is not that there was no forgiveness for the people of old, but that its coming to them was not through those gifts and sacrifices. But the time that was coming 'to set things right' was not yet revealed to them.

It was made manifest in Christ, when he came as 'high priest of the good things that have come'. He is not a high priest merely of hope and promises for the future. In him the promises are fulfilled, the hope has arrived. Yes, there is still room in us for faith and hope yet to be fulfilled (compare Romans 8:18-25), but the victory has already been won for us in him (compare Romans 8:31-39).

The true tent of meeting, the true tabernacle, is in heaven, 'not made with hands (compare 8:5; Exodus 25:9), and Jesus entered it once for all. In truth, the meeting is in him, through him, with him (compare 10:20); and since he is both priest and victim, that is enough to 'obtain eternal redemption'.

God and man both cry 'enough!' in Jesus the peace sacrifice.

THE BLOOD OF THE NEW COVENANT

Hebrews 9:12-22

[12] he entered once for all into the Holy Place, not with the blood of goats and calves, but with his own blood, thus obtaining eternal redemption. [13] For if the blood of goats and bulls, with the sprinkling of the ashes of a heifer, sanctifies those who have been defiled so that their flesh is purified, [14]

55

how much more will the blood of Christ, who through the eternal Spirit offered himself without blemish to God, purify our conscience from dead works to worship the living God! [15] For this reason he is the mediator of a new covenant, so that those who are called may receive the promised eternal inheritance, because a death has occurred that redeems them from the transgressions under the first covenant. [16] Where a will is involved, the death of the one who made it must be established. [17] For a will takes effect only at death, since it is not in force as long as the one who made it is alive. [18] Hence not even the first covenant was inaugurated without blood. [19] For when every commandment had been told to all the people by Moses in accordance with the law, he took the blood of calves and goats, with water and scarlet wool and hyssop, and sprinkled both the scroll itself and all the people, [20] saying, 'This is the blood of the covenant that God has ordained for you.' [21] And in the same way he sprinkled with the blood both the tent and all the vessels used in worship. [22] Indeed, under the law almost everything is purified with blood, and without the shedding of blood there is no forgiveness of sins.

SHEDDING blood touches us with awe, perhaps not as much as it did to those of old, but it does unsettle us too. The truth is that blood is essential to our life, to our being. Let us think for a moment of the blood (unshed) that is quietly circulating now in our veins. Nowadays we know much more about these things than they could have known of old; what our heartbeat is, what blood and breath have to do with each other, and so on.

Well, our factual knowledge about it may be greater than ever before, but our blood is still a marvel, like the stars, a reflection of the glory of our Creator. Blood can still stand as a symbol of each one's life, and of our descent and lineage too, although genes and D.N.A. are the factual favourites for that today. People still talk of blood of kinship. It is no small thing to give blood, nor to 'shed one's blood for freedom' – or for truth. 'Let no one preach', said Morgan

Llwyd, 'any thing other than what they are ready to seal with their blood', as Jesus did.

'With his own blood' it was that Jesus went into the Holy of Holies; that was enough, considering whose blood it was, 'to purify our conscience from dead works to worship the living God'. He did this for us, as he is of the same blood as us (2:14). And he raised the natural living element to be a yet more excellent means of life: 'Drink from it, all of you, for this is my blood of the covenant' (Matthew 26:28; Mark 14:24; compare John 6:52-58).

MEDIATOR OF A NEW COVENANT

Hebrews **9:15-22**

[15] For this reason he is the mediator of a new covenant, so that those who are called may receive the promised eternal inheritance, because a death has occurred that redeems them from the transgressions under the first covenant. [16] Where a will is involved, the death of the one who made it must be established. [17] For a will takes effect only at death, since it is not in force as long as the one who made it is alive. [18] Hence not even the first covenant was inaugurated without blood. [19] For when every commandment had been told to all the people by Moses in accordance with the law, he took the blood of calves and goats, with water and scarlet wool and hyssop, and sprinkled both the scroll itself and all the people, [20] saying, 'This is the blood of the covenant that God has ordained for you.' [21] And in the same way he sprinkled with the blood both the tent and all the vessels used in worship. [22] Indeed, under the law almost everything is purified with blood, and without the shedding of blood there is no forgiveness of sins.

NOW we can say more plainly that Jesus has inaugurated the new covenant; he is the new covenant, as he is high priest and more than high priest. He is Moses and more than

Moses. Jesus is the final sacrifice, the one who is at last fully able to be both from God to the people and for the people to God, the finally sufficient go-between. And he brings this about not by sprinkling the blood of animals, but by shedding his own blood, becoming 'obedient to the point of death – even death on a cross', to win 'the promised eternal inheritance' for his people.

The mention of 'inheritance' brings to mind another use of the Greek word: it can mean 'covenant', yes, but it can also mean 'will' or 'testamentary disposition'. Carrying out a will, a 'last will and testament', will mean the death of the testator, the one who made it. Only thus will the heirs receive what has been left to them. This is used (rather unhistorically) to explain why blood was shed at the making of the old covenant, but the main concern is to convey that Jesus had to die to start the new. One can feel that a pun (in Greek) is a rather superficial turn of argument; but it is a mistake to think that this is offered as a proof. It is rather one way among many of trying to express something that is very near to the heart of the Gospel mystery (we are still in need of 'many and various ways' of expression are we not?).

'Was it not necessary that the Messiah should suffer these things and then enter into his glory?' (Luke 24:25-27, 44-47; compare Acts 3:18, 8:30-35, 17:2-3, 26:22-23). 'When I am lifted up from the earth, I will draw all to myself' (John 12:32).

Open your word to us, Lord; fire our hearts to experience the mystery of your love; give us the grace to live as people who believe in you.

REMOVING SIN BY HIS SACRIFICE (1)

Hebrews 9:23-28

[23] Thus it was necessary for the sketches of the heavenly things to be purified with these rites, but the heavenly things

themselves need better sacrifices than these. [24] For Christ did not enter a sanctuary made by human hands, a mere copy of the true one, but he entered into heaven itself, now to appear in the presence of God on our behalf. [25] Nor was it to offer himself again and again, as the high priest enters the Holy Place year after year with blood that is not his own; [26] for then he would have had to suffer again and again since the foundation of the world. But as it is, he has appeared once for all at the end of the age to remove sin by the sacrifice of himself. [27] And just as it is appointed for mortals to die once, and after that the judgment, [28] so Christ, having been offered once to bear the sins of many, will appear a second time, not to deal with sin, but to save those who are eagerly waiting for him.

THROUGH him and with him and in him, we are brought into the heavenly sanctuary, into the Holy of Holies, into the presence of the Father. This picture fits in with our faith, that he is the Messiah, the fulfilment of all the promises, Son of God. If we use the sanctuary for what it is, an image, a way of thinking about the mystery which is beyond all images, it gives a way for us to approach and appreciate Christ's victory on our behalf.

But when we recall that he won his victory by shedding his blood, by suffering and dying, when we try to take on board that his suffering and dying was no image, but anguish lived in and died in, then surely that is no easier for us 'to take in' than it was for these 'Hebrews' (compare 1 Corinthians 1:23-24, 2:2, 16). It is not only difficult to discern its full meaning; it also carries a personal challenge to each of us who wishes to 'follow him along the way' (Matthew 16:21-26; Mark 8:31-37, 10:52; Luke 9:23, 14:27). As the Welsh hymn has it, *I'll carry the cross, I'll swim the wave, if you but live in me*; well said, and faithful, but too easy to sing.

Why then did Jesus die, rise from the dead, and ascend into heaven? To restore the relationship lost through sin and to ratify the eternal covenant; yes! And as a consequence he was 'declared to be Son of God with power', and given 'all authority in heaven and on earth', to be with us 'always, to the end of the age' (compare Romans 1:4; Matthew 28:18; Revelation 1:17-18). In the days of his flesh, the whole crowd pressed on Jesus in the hope of touching him (compare Luke 6:19), which was difficult; now it is he himself who is in touch with us every one.

REMOVING SIN BY HIS SACRIFICE (2)

Hebrews 9:23-28

[23] Thus it was necessary for the sketches of the heavenly things to be purified with these rites, but the heavenly things themselves need better sacrifices than these. [24] For Christ did not enter a sanctuary made by human hands, a mere copy of the true one, but he entered into heaven itself, now to appear in the presence of God on our behalf. [25] Nor was it to offer himself again and again, as the high priest enters the Holy Place year after year with blood that is not his own; [26] for then he would have had to suffer again and again since the foundation of the world. But as it is, he has appeared once for all at the end of the age to remove sin by the sacrifice of himself. [27] And just as it is appointed for mortals to die once, and after that the judgment, [28] so Christ, having been offered once to bear the sins of many, will appear a second time, not to deal with sin, but to save those who are eagerly waiting for him.

THE 'sanctuary made by human hands' we are told, is 'a mere copy of the true one', modelled on the pattern given to Moses on the mountain; the furnishing and instruments were mere 'sketches of the heavenly things'. And yet in fact the picture of the heavenly sanctuary and its contents is a projection of the earthly things, an earthly image offered as an aid to thinking of heaven. Heaven itself is not less real than the earthly Temple; the heavenly sacrifice is not less real than the earthly sacrifices. We can be tempted to feel they are less real because we naturally think in images, but no; we are to realise that the whole of heaven is greater than any image or thought can say. There is no image that can present it as it is.

All the same, if we put our imagination to work, we have here an excellent picture that suggests much more than it depicts. 'The heavenly things' are not some sort of tools, but the relationship with God now restored after being blocked by sin. 'For Christ did not enter a sanctuary made by human hands, a mere copy of the true one, but he entered into heaven itself, now to appear in the presence of God on our behalf.' Where is heaven? Come to think of it, it is here, 'a heartbeat away'. 'God is everywhere.' No journey is needed, no going, only to pass through the veil – which is the image we are offered of what Jesus has done (compare 10:20).

Jesus' death has been once for all, 'at the end of the age, to remove sin by the sacrifice of himself'; and that final salvation is offered us not from afar, but here – from the other side of the veil, indeed – but from nearer than any image can convey. Have we not immediate reason to thank him?

Letter to the Hebrews

Chapter 10

[1] Since the law has only a shadow of the good things to come and not the true form of these realities, it can never, by the same sacrifices that are continually offered year after year, make perfect those who approach. [2] Otherwise, would they not have ceased being offered, since the worshipers, cleansed once for all, would no longer have any consciousness of sin? [3] But in these sacrifices there is a reminder of sin year after year. [4] For it is impossible for the blood of bulls and goats to take away sins. [5] Consequently, when Christ came into the world, he said, 'Sacrifices and offerings you have not desired, but a body you have prepared for me; [6] in burnt offerings and sin offerings you have taken no pleasure. [7] Then I said, "See, God, I have come to do your will, O God" (in the scroll of the book it is written of me).' [8] When he said above, 'You have neither desired nor taken pleasure in sacrifices and offerings and burnt offerings and sin offerings' (these are offered according to the law), [9] then he added, 'See, I have come to do your will.' He abolishes the first in order to establish the second. [10] And it is by God's will that we have been sanctified through the offering of the body of Jesus Christ once for all. [11] And every priest stands day after day at his service, offering again and again the same sacrifices that can never take away sins. [12] But when Christ had offered for all time a single sacrifice for sins, 'he sat down at the right hand of God,' [13] and since then has been waiting 'until his enemies would be made a footstool for his feet.' [14] For by a single offering he has perfected for all time those who are sanctified. [15] And the Holy Spirit also testifies to us, for after saying, [16] 'This is the covenant that I will make with them after those days, says the Lord: I will put

my laws in their hearts, and I will write them on their minds,' [17] he also adds, 'I will remember their sins and their lawless deeds no more.' [18] Where there is forgiveness of these, there is no longer any offering for sin. [19] Therefore, my friends, since we have confidence to enter the sanctuary by the blood of Jesus, [20] by the new and living way that he opened for us through the curtain (that is, through his flesh), [21] and since we have a great priest over the house of God, [22] let us approach with a true heart in full assurance of faith, with our hearts sprinkled clean from an evil conscience and our bodies washed with pure water. [23] Let us hold fast to the confession of our hope without wavering, for he who has promised is faithful. [24] And let us consider how to provoke one another to love and good deeds, [25] not neglecting to meet together, as is the habit of some, but encouraging one another, and all the more as you see the Day approaching. [26] For if we wilfully persist in sin after having received the knowledge of the truth, there no longer remains a sacrifice for sins, [27] but a fearful prospect of judgment, and a fury of fire that will consume the adversaries. [28] Anyone who has violated the law of Moses dies without mercy 'on the testimony of two or three witnesses.' [29] How much worse punishment do you think will be deserved by those who have spurned the Son of God, profaned the blood of the covenant by which they were sanctified, and outraged the Spirit of grace? [30] For we know the one who said, 'Vengeance is mine, I will repay.' And again, 'The Lord will judge his people.' [31] It is a fearful thing to fall into the hands of the living God. [32] But recall those earlier days when, after you had been enlightened, you endured a hard struggle with sufferings, [33] sometimes being publicly exposed to abuse and persecution, and sometimes being partners with those so treated. [34] For you had compassion for those who were in prison, and you cheerfully accepted the plundering of your possessions, knowing that you yourselves possessed something better and more lasting. [35] Do not, therefore, abandon that confidence of yours; it brings a great reward. [36] For you need endurance, so that when you have done the will of God, you may receive what was promised. [37] For yet 'in a very little while, the one who is coming will come and will not delay; [38] but my righteous one will live by faith. My soul takes no pleasure in anyone who shrinks back.' [39] But we are not among those who shrink back and so are lost, but among those who have faith and so are saved.

CHRIST'S ONE SACRIFICE
FULLY SUFFICIENT (1)

Hebrews **10:1-4**

[1] Since the law has only a shadow of the good things to come and not the true form of these realities, it can never, by the same sacrifices that are continually offered year after year, make perfect those who approach. [2] Otherwise, would they not have ceased being offered, since the worshipers, cleansed once for all, would no longer have any consciousness of sin? [3] But in these sacrifices there is a reminder of sin year after year. [4] For it is impossible for the blood of bulls and goats to take away sins.

NOW there is no more need to repeat the old sacrifices for sin; they were no more than a foreshadowing 'of the blessings that were to come'. If they had been sufficient, the worshippers would not have needed to repeat the sacrifices from year to year.

At first sight, this seems to ignore the fact that people sin again, and so need repeated forgiveness and reconciliation. But isn't this the point, that ritual forgiveness, ritual cleansing, is all that could be expected from ritual sacrifice? What was needed was 'worship in spirit and in truth'.

Jesus' suffering and death and resurrection (along with his ascension from history into glory) opened for us once and for ever access to 'the throne of grace'. Jesus' mission is accomplished, but our approach to that throne of grace occurs in our time, in which we are 'to receive mercy and find grace to help in time of need' (4:16). In history, his saving work was before our time: 'while we still were sinners Christ died for us', and 'if while we were enemies, we were reconciled to God through the death of his Son, much more surely, having been reconciled, will we be saved by his life' (compare Romans 5:6-11). In mystery, our access to it is now; not only in ritual, but in sacrament.

We have already been reconciled in Jesus. But we need now and always to tune in to what he has achieved for us, to rise again from our falls (compare Proverbs 4:16). That is why we say daily, 'forgive us our sins / our debts / our trespasses' (Luke 11:4; Matthew 6:12). Jesus is with us in our weakness, to offer us forgiveness when we truly repent. And he takes our inadequate offering of ourselves into his one sacrifice.

CHRIST'S ONE SACRIFICE
FULLY SUFFICIENT (2)

Hebrews **10:5-10**

[5] Consequently, when Christ came into the world, he said, 'Sacrifices and offerings you have not desired, but a body you have prepared for me; [6] in burnt offerings and sin offerings you have taken no pleasure. [7] Then I said, "See, God, I have come to do your will, O God" (in the scroll of the book it is written of me).' [8] When he said above, 'You have neither desired nor taken pleasure in sacrifices and offerings and burnt offerings and sin offerings' (these are offered according to the law), [9] then he added, 'See, I have come to do your will.' He abolishes the first in order to establish the second. [10] And it is by God's will that we have been sanctified through the offering of the body of Jesus Christ once for all.

THE Psalm (40:5-8) expresses the heart of worship: human beings cannot ever grasp or express the full range of wonders that God has accomplished for us. The ritual sacrifices of the Law cannot serve as an adequate response to those wonders. The key is obedience to God (compare 1 Samuel 15:22-23). To give oneself wholly to the Lord, to love him with all one's heart and soul and strength (compare Mark 12:29-33; Matthew 9:13), that will do it – but which of us is up to doing that? Only one of us, to tell the truth; and so, says our author, it is that one of us who really says this, not the Psalmist but Jesus, 'as he came into the world'. It is he who offers the true worship that the human heart at its best longs to offer.

Here am I, 'I have come to do your will, O God'; here am I, in place of all 'the sacrifices and offerings and burnt-offerings and sin-offerings'. 'And it is by that will of God that we have been sanctified', brought near to God, enabled to be one with God, 'through the offering of the body of Jesus Christ once for all'. Yes; and in the prayer where Jesus says this on his own behalf, he says: 'for their sakes I sanctify myself, so that they also may be sanctified in truth' (John 17:19).

That is how he brings us in our time into his true worship, by consecrating our present offering of ourselves to make it one with him.

Through him and with him and in him, in the unity of the Holy Spirit, all glory and honour is yours, almighty Father, for ever and ever.

NEW COVENANT, NEW PRIEST

Hebrews **10:11-18**

[11] And every priest stands day after day at his service, offering again and again the same sacrifices that can never take away sins. [12] But when Christ had offered for all time a single sacrifice for sins, 'he sat down at the right hand of God,' [13] and since then has been waiting 'until his enemies would be made a footstool for his feet.' [14] For by a single offering he has perfected for all time those who are sanctified. [15] And

the Holy Spirit also testifies to us, for after saying, [16] 'This is the covenant that I will make with them after those days, says the Lord: I will put my laws in their hearts, and I will write them on their minds,' [17] he also adds, 'I will remember their sins and their lawless deeds no more.' [18] Where there is forgiveness of these, there is no longer any offering for sin.

THE former priests stood 'day after day... offering again and again the same sacrifices that can never take away sins.' This priest, Jesus, having offered 'for all time a single sacrifice for sins', 'sat down at the right hand of God'.

His victory is won; 'I have conquered the world' (John 16:33). Jesus is the first fruits, now waiting for the whole harvest to be brought home, 'until he has put all his enemies under his feet' (compare 1 Corinthians 15:22-26). 'By a single offering he has perfected for all time those who are sanctified' from generation to generation.

The promise of a new covenant includes both putting the Law into each heart and mind, and remembering sins and lawless deeds no more. Forgiveness is already there on God's side, and God offers it to us, calling us on behalf of Christ to be reconciled to God (compare 2 Corinthians 5:14-15, 18-21).

Jesus is the Temple, the priest and the victim, 'able to save completely those who approach God through him, since he always lives to make intercession for them'. There he is, full of mercy, if only we turn to him; but turn to him we must.

O my God, give me the grace to repent, to turn more and more to you; grant me the forgiveness won for me by Jesus Christ your Son, and the help of your Spirit to keep me in your love through all my days.

APPROACHING GOD IN CHRIST

Hebrews 10:19-25

[19] Therefore, my friends, since we have confidence to enter the sanctuary by the blood of Jesus, [20] by the new and living way that he opened for us through the curtain (that is, through his flesh), [21] and since we have a great priest over the house of God, [22] let us approach with a true heart in full assurance of faith, with our hearts sprinkled clean from an evil conscience and our bodies washed with pure water. [23] Let us hold fast to the confession of our hope without wavering, for he who has promised is faithful. [24] And let us consider how to provoke one another to love and good deeds, [25] not neglecting to meet together, as is the habit of some, but encouraging one another, and all the more as you see the Day approaching.

IN the new order, our high priest is not the only one who may go into the heavenly sanctuary. Now 'we have confidence to enter the sanctuary by the blood of Jesus, by the new and living way that he opened for us through the curtain, (that is, through his flesh)'. His body is the way, by being offered (10:10). He himself is the way: 'I am the way, and the truth, and the life' (John 14:6).

Not from any merit of ours, but 'since we have a great high priest over the house of God, let us approach with a true heart in full assurance of faith, with our hearts sprinkled clean from an evil conscience and our bodies washed with pure water'. As the priests of the old Temple were expected to be ritually clean and ready to carry out their service, so Christ's faithful are expected to prepare within and without (being baptized) for joining in his sacrifice.

Living as a disciple demands perseverance: 'Let us hold fast to the confession of our hope without wavering, for he who has promised us is faithful.' Disciples are to give each other and receive from each other considerate advice and support, provoking one another 'to love and good deeds'.

So we are not to neglect our meeting together, our own *synagogue* (which is a pledge of 'our being gathered together to him'; compare 2 Thessalonians 2:1; Matthew 18:20). Indeed the Word and the Spirit are in every heart, but they bind everyone to one another and to the Father, in Christ Jesus.

A FURTHER WARNING
NOT TO TURN BACK

Hebrews 10:26-31

[26] For if we wilfully persist in sin after having received the knowledge of the truth, there no longer remains a sacrifice for sins, [27] but a fearful prospect of judgment, and a fury of fire that will consume the adversaries. [28] Anyone who has violated the law of Moses dies without mercy 'on the testimony of two or three witnesses.' [29] How much worse punishment do you think will be deserved by those who have spurned the Son of God, profaned the blood of the covenant by which they were sanctified, and outraged the Spirit of grace? [30] For we know the one who said, 'Vengeance is mine, I will repay.' And again, 'The Lord will judge his people.' [31] It is a fearful thing to fall into the hands of the living God.

'IF we wilfully persist in sin after having received the knowledge of the truth, there no longer remains a sacrifice for sins'. If we reject Christ's sacrifice having truly welcomed the truth, that is knowing that it is the only sacrifice for sins, what sacrifice for sins can we have recourse to? The prospect is terrifying. However, John Chrysostom tells us: 'What is said here is neither "there is no more room to repent", nor "there is no more forgiveness to be had", but "there is no further sacrifice", that is "there is no further Cross" '. Jesus cannot be crucified again (compare 6:6).

The purpose of the *Hebrews*-author's warning of 'a fearful prospect of judgement, and a fury of fire that will consume the adversaries' is to waken the audience and encourage them to repent, so that they do not sin any more but rather seek to arrive more closely at their place in Christ. It is surely that, rather than announcing a condemnation of anyone. All the same, why do we tend to think of that sort of threatening sermon as old-fashioned? Perhaps the way this picture has been used in the past was too sweeping and lacking in mercy (we need to recall how Daniel Rowland had to be reminded to preach mercy and forgiveness as well as hellfire, and St. John Vianney had a similar lesson to learn). None the less, does the warning not stand? Not against weakness and mistakes, indeed, but against the blind and not-so-blind stubbornness that is aware of the light and rejects it. In our day we have had ample experience of 'man's (diabolical) inhumanity to man', of the manifold possibilities of self-deception, and also of diminished responsibility to some degree. 'Father, forgive them, for they know not what they do.'

Lord never let me separate myself from you.

ENCOURAGEMENT TO PERSEVERE

Hebrews 10:26-39

[26] For if we wilfully persist in sin after having received the knowledge of the truth, there no longer remains a sacrifice for sins, [27] but a fearful prospect of judgment, and a fury of fire that will consume the adversaries. [28] Anyone who has violated the law of Moses dies without mercy 'on the testimony of two or three witnesses.' [29] How much worse punishment do you think will be deserved by those who have spurned the Son of God, profaned the blood of the covenant by which they were sanctified, and outraged the Spirit of grace? [30] For we know the one who said, 'Vengeance is

mine, I will repay.' And again, 'The Lord will judge his people.' [31] It is a fearful thing to fall into the hands of the living God. [32] But recall those earlier days when, after you had been enlightened, you endured a hard struggle with sufferings, [33] sometimes being publicly exposed to abuse and persecution, and sometimes being partners with those so treated. [34] For you had compassion for those who were in prison, and you cheerfully accepted the plundering of your possessions, knowing that you yourselves possessed something better and more lasting. [35] Do not, therefore, abandon that confidence of yours; it brings a great reward. [36] For you need endurance, so that when you have done the will of God, you may receive what was promised. [37] For yet 'in a very little while, the one who is coming will come and will not delay; [38] but my righteous one will live by faith. My soul takes no pleasure in anyone who shrinks back.' [39] But we are not among those who shrink back and so are lost, but among those who have faith and so are saved.

FIRST a taste of the cane, and now consolation; and that because of the faithfulness the 'Hebrews' have already shown. After their first conversion and their baptism, their enlightenment, they faced afflictions firmly, 'sometimes being publicly exposed to abuse and persecution, and sometimes being partners with those so treated'. They had compassion for those in prison, and cheerfully accepted being deprived of their possessions, knowing as they did that they 'possessed something better and more lasting'. What was that? Their true selves, already being realised in faith (compare Luke 9:24), and fulfilled in lasting love (1 Corinthians 13:13).

This is not the time to lose the reward for that great struggle; what is needed now is endurance, doing the will of God so as to receive what was promised: 'In a very little while, the one who is coming will come and will not delay; but my righteous one will live by faith'. Shrinking back gives no pleasure to God. God is love and light, and in him there is no darkness; we must not stay in our darkness, but come into God's light.

'But we are not among those who shrink back and are lost, but among those who have faith and so that… we may live with him' (1 Thessalonians 5:9-10).

Letter to the Hebrews

Chapter 11

[1] Now faith is the assurance of things hoped for, the conviction of things not seen. [2] Indeed, by faith our ancestors received approval. [3] By faith we understand that the worlds were prepared by the word of God, so that what is seen was made from things that are not visible. [4] By faith Abel offered to God a more acceptable sacrifice than Cain's. Through this he received approval as righteous, God himself giving approval to his gifts; he died, but through his faith he still speaks. [5] By faith Enoch was taken so that he did not experience death; and 'he was not found, because God had taken him.' For it was attested before he was taken away that 'he had pleased God.' [6] And without faith it is impossible to please God, for whoever would approach him must believe that he exists and that he rewards those who seek him. [7] By faith Noah, warned by God about events as yet unseen, respected the warning and built an ark to save his household; by this he condemned the world and became an heir to the righteousness that is in accordance with faith. [8] By faith Abraham obeyed when he was called to set out for a place that he was to receive as an inheritance; and he set out, not knowing where he was going. [9] By faith he stayed for a time in the land he had been promised, as in a foreign land, living in tents, as did Isaac and Jacob, who were heirs with him of the same promise. [10] For he looked forward to the city that has foundations, whose architect and builder is God. [11] By faith he received power of procreation, even though he was too old – and Sarah herself was barren – because he considered him faithful who had promised. [12] Therefore from one person, and this one as good as dead, descendants were born, 'as many as the stars of heaven and

as the innumerable grains of sand by the seashore.' [13] All of these died in faith without having received the promises, but from a distance they saw and greeted them. They confessed that they were strangers and foreigners on the earth, [14] for people who speak in this way make it clear that they are seeking a homeland. [15] If they had been thinking of the land that they had left behind, they would have had opportunity to return. [16] But as it is, they desire a better country, that is, a heavenly one. Therefore God is not ashamed to be called their God; indeed, he has prepared a city for them. [17] By faith Abraham, when put to the test, offered up Isaac. He who had received the promises was ready to offer up his only son, [18] of whom he had been told, 'It is through Isaac that descendants shall be named for you.' [19] He considered the fact that God is able even to raise someone from the dead – and figuratively speaking, he did receive him back. [20] By faith Isaac invoked blessings for the future on Jacob and Esau. [21] By faith Jacob, when dying, blessed each of the sons of Joseph, 'bowing in worship over the top of his staff.' [22] By faith Joseph, at the end of his life, made mention of the exodus of the Israelites and gave instructions about his burial. [23] By faith Moses was hidden by his parents for three months after his birth, because they saw that the child was beautiful; and they were not afraid of the king's edict. [24] By faith Moses, when he was grown up, refused to be called a son of Pharaoh's daughter, [25] choosing rather to share ill-treatment with the people of God than to enjoy the fleeting pleasures of sin. [26] He considered abuse suffered for the Christ to be greater wealth than the treasures of Egypt, for he was looking ahead to the reward. [27] By faith he left Egypt, unafraid of the king's anger; for he persevered as though he saw him who is invisible. [28] By faith he kept the Passover and the sprinkling of blood, so that the destroyer of the firstborn would not touch the firstborn of Israel. [29] By faith the people passed through the Red Sea as if it were dry land, but when the Egyptians attempted to do so they were drowned. [30] By faith the walls of Jericho fell after they had been encircled for seven days. [31] By faith Rahab the prostitute did not perish with those who were disobedient, because she had received the spies in peace. [32] And what more should I say? For time would fail me to tell of Gideon, Barak, Samson, Jephthah, of David and Samuel and the prophets – [33] who through faith conquered kingdoms, administered justice, obtained promises, shut the mouths of lions, [34] quenched raging fire, escaped the edge of the sword, won strength out of weakness, became mighty in war, put foreign armies to flight. [35] Women received their dead by resurrection. Others were tortured, refusing to accept release, in order to obtain a better resurrection. [36] Others suffered mocking and flogging, and even chains and imprisonment. [37] They were stoned to death, they were sawn in two, they were killed by the sword; they went about in skins of sheep and goats, destitute, persecuted, tormented – [38] of whom the world was not worthy. They wandered in deserts and mountains, and in caves and holes in the ground. [39] Yet all these, though they were commended for their faith, did not receive what was promised, [40] since God had provided something better so that they would not, apart from us, be made perfect.

FAITH

Hebrews **11:1-2**

[1] Now faith is the assurance of things hoped for, the conviction of things not seen. [2] Indeed, by faith our ancestors received approval.

IF faith is the key, let us consider what it has been and still is. And the first remark is that it is a sort of self-giving that has been found in God's people ever since the beginning of the world. This is a deeper truth than the insufficiency of the Law, and far older than the Law itself.

We have here a development of the first verses of the *Letter*. God revealed himself to people of old 'in many and various ways', awakening in them a faithful response to the light he was giving them. Now the people of old include not just 'our ancestors' but all whom God drew towards his light. Having now revealed himself 'in a Son', he has presented the object of faith more fully, but the same basic response is invited as has always been.

Faith, a present reality, has to do with the future and with what is unseen. It is 'the assurance of things hoped for', a present affirmation that they will be given, and 'the conviction of things not seen', a proof that they are real. 'One can suppose', says St John Chrysostom, 'that the objects of hope are unreal because they are not present; so faith gives them their reality, or rather, faith is their present reality.' To have what you do not have, to know what is yet unseen: that is the achievement, which is a gift and a grace (compare Romans 8:24-27).

'Indeed, by faith our ancestors received approval', by the Word of God. Where of old there was a call to 'sing the praises of famous men, our ancestors in their generations' for their mighty achievements (Sirach/Ecclesiasticus 44:1) – which did mean celebrating the gifts of the Lord – here our author changes the emphasis: it was by faith that they won a good name, and that by God's gift.

FAITH IN A CREATOR

Hebrews 11:3

[3] By faith we understand that the worlds were prepared by the word of God, so that what is seen was made from things that are not visible.

EARTH and sky, land and sea and all that is on them and in them, people and their world and history, our hates and loves, everything that is within the horizon of human observation, thought, and action: all that and more is a manifold wonder that does not force anyone to think that there is anything beyond it. It is possible (but not necessary!) to think that the whole thing is the result of countless chances and accidents that lack any sense; that there is no further significance beyond what human capacities can find.

For the ear of faith, the eye of faith, it is not so: 'The heavens are telling the glory of God; and the firmament proclaims his handiwork. Day to day pours forth speech, and night to night declares knowledge. There is no speech, nor are there words; their voice is not heard; yet their voice goes out through all the earth and their words to the end of the world' (Psalm 19:1-4). And again: 'He spoke, and it came to be; he commanded, and it stood firm' (Psalm 33:6-9).

'By faith we understand that the worlds were prepared by the word of God, so that what is seen was made from things that are not visible.' Human understanding, directed and awakened by faith, is able to discern that there is behind and within and above the whole world 'the Giver of being, the generous Supporter, the Ruler of all that is' (Ann Griffiths: compare Romans 1:19-20; Wisdom 13:1-9).

THE FAITH OF ABEL

Hebrews **11:4**

[4] By faith Abel offered to God a more acceptable sacrifice than Cain's. Through this he received approval as righteous, God himself giving approval to his gifts; he died, but through his faith he still speaks.

'RIGHTEOUS Abel' is named as the first just man to be murdered (Matthew 23:35). It is said that 'the Lord had regard for Abel and his offerings' (Gen 4:5), but why? That is not directly explained; it could be because Abel 'did well' (compare 4:7). Our author's interpretation takes it deeper: 'By faith Abel offered to God a more acceptable sacrifice than Cain's; through this he received approval as righteous, God himself giving approval to his gifts.' Once our attention is drawn, we notice what is said in Genesis: that Abel brought 'of the firstlings of his flock, their fat portions' (4:3); and so it is reasonable to take such generosity as a sign of a truly thankful heart aware of dependence on God, with the hint that Cain's offering was not in the same spirit.

Our author's concern here is not with history, but with proper relationship with the Lord. And we are invited to read the story in the light of the Gospel, reasoning like this: (a) in declaring that Abel's sacrifice is better, the Lord declares that Abel is pleasing to him; (b) it is only by faith that one can be pleasing to the Lord; (c) therefore it was that faith which made Abel's sacrifice better than his brother's. What is this faith then? It is what his sacrifice expressed: his readiness to give what he treasured most, losing the best he had of visible good in order to worship the invisible, and that without tangible present reward. And so, though 'he died … he still speaks' (compare Gen 4:10); because the Lord accepts him (compare Luke 9:24; 12:44).

THE FAITH OF ENOCH

Hebrews 11:5-6

[5] By faith Enoch was taken so that he did not experience death; and 'he was not found, because God had taken him.' For it was attested before he was taken away that 'he had pleased God.' [6] And without faith it is impossible to please God, for whoever would approach him must believe that he exists and that he rewards those who seek him.

SIMILARLY, the saying that Enoch 'pleased God' (Wisdom 4:10) and that he 'walked with God' (Genesis 5:24) amounts to saying that he did so by faith, because that is the only way that can be done. This faith means believing two truths: that God exists, and 'that he rewards those who seek him'. 'Whoever would approach him must believe that he exists…', recognizing that God is the source and home of all good that is worth having' (compare Exodus 3:14; Hebrews

10:35; Psalm 16:2). This again says nothing about what idea of God Enoch had or could have had, but that the one God truly drew Enoch to himself. This may be a comfort for us when we think of our good friends who think they do not believe in God.

Approaching God (as Enoch is said to have walked with him) echoes the talk of approaching God through Jesus (7:25). The track of the faithful of the old covenant is discerned to have the same basic pattern as those of the new, with one difference. Without knowing in this world about Jesus, it was possible to approach God. Still that was not without Jesus, in the eternal plan and purpose. He is the way to the Father, and all who come to the Father come by him, though they know it not in this world. In virtue of the promise that was conveyed 'in many and various ways', it was and is through him that people found and find the way to faith (compare John 1:9-13; 3:8).

A living faith, directed towards the true and living God, is kindled by God himself; he invites us to seek him seriously (compare Acts 17:27), not with our heads alone but from our hearts, from a love that tries to walk in the light (compare 1 John 4:7-8). We too can 'go astray while seeking God and desiring to find him' (Wisdom 13:6-9); so let us ask for the grace to set our mind and heart most truly on him, because he is our 'very great reward' (Genesis 15:1).

NOAH'S FAITH

Hebrews **11:7**

[7] By faith Noah, warned by God about events as yet unseen, respected the warning and built an ark to save his household; by this he condemned the world and became an heir to the righteousness that is in accordance with faith.

NOAH is famous for being a righteous man, 'blameless in his generation', who, when others were corrupt, 'walked with God' (Genesis 6:9-12). He is famous also for the Ark in which he and his family and all those creatures escaped the Flood, so that life could continue on the earth (compare Sirach 44:17). In other places (for example Matthew 24:37--38), the story of what happened to everyone else is used as a warning. Here the emphasis is on Noah's faith.

Warned by God of something that was as yet unseen, Noah built an ark to save his family. In doing so he expressed his faith, showed up everyone else's lack of faith, and by the same token was given the divine approval that is won by faith.

In the story Noah prepares for a particular crisis, though it is a crisis that threatens the whole world. Warning that the end of the world is nigh has become associated with marginal groups who have named the date so often and then have had to cope with one disappointment after another. On another front, there is plainly an interest in fictional final calamities, sometimes touched by not so fictional scientific forecasts. But we are not to be unduly upset about dates or calamities. The warning to us is for us to be ready, 'for the Son of Man is coming at an unexpected hour' (Matthew 24:44). Perhaps the call will come to me tonight. There is no need any more to make an ark. One is already available, invisible, not a ship but the Son, Emmanuel.

ABRAHAM'S FAITH (1)

Hebrews 11:8-10

[8] By faith Abraham obeyed when he was called to set out for a place that he was to receive as an inheritance; and he set out, not knowing where he was going. [9] By faith he stayed for a time in the land he had been promised, as in a foreign land, living in tents, as did Isaac and Jacob, who were heirs with him of the same promise. [10] For he looked forward to the city that has foundations, whose architect and builder is God.

WITH the call to Abraham and his obedience to it we reach the beginning of the Lord's plan to raise a people for himself as a means to extend his blessings to the whole world. And in the first challenge to Abraham we find a pattern that comes into play time and again in the history of this people, and, in several ways, in the history of everyone who seriously seeks to grow near to God.

The call is astonishing: what could the voice in the night (or howsoever) mean to a man of seventy-five who has spent his life so far in a society that worships many gods? The call is for Abraham to 'Go from your country and your kindred and your father's house to the land that I will show you' (Genesis 12:1), without saying yet where to. And the response of faith is also astonishing: 'and he set out, not knowing where he was going'.

Isaiah offers the same reply before hearing where he is to be sent: 'Here am I, send me!' (Isaiah 6:8); and the same challenge is offered the people of Israel to restore them to the covenant: 'I will lead the blind by a road they do not know, by paths they have not known I will guide them' (Isaiah 42:16; compare 6:9-10). As Saunders Lewis has said, 'The daily life of faith is to walk as one who sees through the darkness of the blind'.

John of the Cross also takes up this theme: 'To reach where you know not, you must go by the way you know not. To reach what you do not own, you must go by a way you do not own. To reach what you are not, you must go by the way you are not'. Exactly so, Abraham lived in the Promised Land not as its owner, but in tents, looking forward to the city 'whose architect and builder is God'. The Christian has need of the same spirit (compare 1 Corinthians 7:29-31!).

CHILD OF FAITH

Hebrews **11:11-12**

[11] By faith he received power of procreation, even though he was too old – and Sarah herself was barren – because he considered him faithful who had promised. [12] Therefore from one person, and this one as good as dead, descendants were born, 'as many as the stars of heaven and as the innumerable grains of sand by the seashore.'

SARAH was barren, and both she and Abraham were very old anyway. It's no surprise that Sarah and Abraham are both said to have laughed (*Isaac*) on hearing the promise that they were going to have a child (Genesis 17:17; 18:12--15; 21:1-7). The promise was beyond any natural expectation, and its fulfilment was to show God's power at its utmost in human powerlessness (compare 2 Corinthians 12:9!). Their acceptance of the promise was an act of faith, in that they both 'considered him faithful who had promised'. By their faithful consent the Lord began to implement the plan, to raise 'descendants as many as the stars of heaven and as the innumerable grains of sand by the seashore'.

'He gives the barren woman a home, making her the joyous mother of children' (Psalm 113:9). The pattern is repeated from generation to generation with one woman after another: with Hannah, mother of Samuel (1 Samuel 1:2--2:10); with the Shunammite (2 Kings 4:14-17); with Elizabeth, mother of John the Baptist (Luke 1:7); and in another way with Mary, mother of Jesus (Luke 1:34-35). It comes into play also to express the wonderful forgiveness of the whole people and their restoration to the covenant (Isaiah 54:1-10). And one can say that the proper human response to the marvel of divine generosity in every case is a living faith that goes into action.

Perhaps I, perhaps we are sometimes too ready to lose heart because of our weakness and our many failings, and sometimes because we have too large a notion of our abilities.

Perhaps the big *I*, the big *We*, has to become less so that his grace may have a chance to work in us and through us (compare John 3:30).

SEEKING A HOMELAND

Hebrews 11:13-16

[13] All of these died in faith without having received the promises, but from a distance they saw and greeted them. They confessed that they were strangers and foreigners on the earth, [14] for people who speak in this way make it clear that they are seeking a homeland. [15] If they had been thinking of the land that they had left behind, they would have had opportunity to return. [16] But as it is, they desire a better country, that is, a heavenly one. Therefore God is not ashamed to be called their God; indeed, he has prepared a city for them.

ABRAHAM and Sarah, Isaac and Jacob, as they had lived, 'died in faith without having received the promises, but from a distance they saw and greeted them', looking ahead from the midst of the current concerns, 'as one sees the harbour from far off and rejoices already at the sight' (John Chrysostom); 'where your treasure is, there your heart will be also' (Matthew 6:21).

They often admit that they are 'strangers and foreigners on the earth' (Genesis 23:4; Exodus 2:22; 1 Chronicles 29:15; Psalm 39:12). They were not 'thinking of the land they had left behind; that would not have been so difficult to go back to. The truth is, 'they desire a better country, that is, a heavenly one. Therefore God is not ashamed to be called their God; indeed, he has prepared a city for them', a place to dwell and be a community.

Although the promises have been fulfilled in Christ Jesus, they have not yet been wholly fulfilled in us. So our situation is not altogether different from that of those people of old; presently (Hebrews 13:14) we too shall be told that 'here we have no lasting city, but we are looking for the city that is to come' (compare 2 Corinthians 5:1-10; 1 Peter 1:1; 2:11).

If we are to follow their example of faith, this does not mean that we should not work in this world for justice and peace, but the very contrary. It is exactly by dealing kindly with our neighbours, whoever they be, that we will belong already to the community of heaven (Ephesians 2:19-22; compare John 13:35). But it does mean that we live by aims and standards and values that are not confined to this world.

ABRAHAM'S FAITH (2)

Hebrews **11:17-19**

[17] By faith Abraham, when put to the test, offered up Isaac. He who had received the promises was ready to offer up his only son, [18] of whom he had been told, 'It is through Isaac that descendants shall be named for you.' [19] He considered the fact that God is able even to raise someone from the dead – and figuratively speaking, he did receive him back.

SO, Abraham already had an heir, and an outstanding promise of descendants, plenty to please the heart of an old patriarch. And then, like a quiet thunderbolt: 'Take your son, your only son Isaac, whom you love, and go to the land of Moriah, and offer him there as a burnt-offering on one of the mountains that I shall show you' (Gen 22:2). Would we not hesitate: could it be the voice of God that asked for such a deed? Granting that God the Creator is lord of life and death, even so would this command mean that God was contradicting himself, reneging on his promise? What a test of Abraham's faith! The father who had so gladly welcomed the promises, faced now with a final disappointment, the loss of the last chance to become 'a great nation' (Genesis 12:2).

But 'by faith' it was that Abraham, 'put to the test, offered up Isaac' – either total foolishness or faith to be 'ready to offer up his only son'. The story does not give much help towards explaining Abraham's mind, but perhaps it gives enough: a ready 'Here I am' each time in face of the test and in face of its resolution; 'God himself will provide the lamb for a burnt-offering, my son', and then the quiet move towards doing the deed until he's told not to lay his hand on the boy (Genesis 22:1-14).

Our author of *Hebrews* offers another reason, namely that Abraham had considered 'that God is able even to raise someone from the dead – and figuratively speaking, he did receive him back'. This surely brings us to the central mystery of the Gospel: 'He did not withhold his own Son …' (Romans 8:32; compare John 3:16; 1 John 4:9).

FAITH FROM AGE TO AGE (1)

Hebrews 11:20

[20] By faith Isaac invoked blessings for the future on Jacob and Esau.

A very human series of events is displayed in the struggles between Jacob and Esau and their descendants. Jacob won priority and blessing by taking advantage of his brother's weakness; none the less, it was Jacob who won, to the disappointment of Isaac and yet according to God's plan. So it took faith on Isaac's part, we are told, to suffer the result of the trick and accept that Jacob was the Lord's choice rather than his brother. We may well suppose that he found that acceptance costly (Genesis 27-28:5; Romans 9:10-14; compare Mark 10:40; Matthew 20:23!). So it was, anyhow, that 'by faith Isaac invoked blessings for the future on Jacob and Esau', not only for their own future, but for what was yet to come.

It is hard enough to put up with what disappoints my own wishes, in matters small or great; but when the kingdom of God is at stake, respect for truth, true devotion, or justice and peace, it can be very difficult to accept what is to my mind being done in a less than correct way. I need to remember, costly as it may be, that the cause is God's, that the future is his, and that his ways are not our ways (Isaiah 55:8-9).

I may have to refuse to go along with what my conscience tells me I shouldn't, but maybe I should be ready to allow that what I cannot change may be after all before God fruitful for good. How many parents have experienced this with their children? And what about disagreements among Christians with regard to furthering the Kingdom? (Philippians 1. 15-19).

FAITH FROM AGE TO AGE (2)

Hebrews **11:21-22**

[21] By faith Jacob, when dying, blessed each of the sons of Joseph, 'bowing in worship over the top of his staff.' [22] By faith Joseph, at the end of his life, made mention of the exodus of the Israelites and gave instructions about his burial.

PASSING on the blessing at the time of death meant recognizing that the promises had not yet been fulfilled, and expressing faith that they would be in the future. This time, too, it is the youngest who gets the first blessing, unexpected by his father (Genesis 48), and Joseph receives the priority promised him, but in an unexpected way, that his sons have it rather than he himself (48:22; compare 37:1--11). Faith means a readiness to take on board again a truth higher than we think: 'my thoughts are not your thoughts, nor are your ways my ways' (Isaiah 55:8-11).

When Joseph's turn came to die, he affirmed – in spite of all his own success and for all the welcome they received in

Egypt at that time – that Egypt would not be a lasting home for the children of Israel (Genesis 50:22-26). By faith he continued to speak of going forth to the Promised Land, and of not leaving even his bones in Egypt.

The world we live in sets its heart on success, as near immediate success as possible. Waiting breeds impatience, always feels longer; and the longest wait is when hope is deferred to the next generation, and the next again. That won't do. Anyhow, what is success? A comfortable life the way we want it, food and drink and sex, and plenty of resources, along with safety from the anger and lusts of other people. That notion of success is not uncommon in our world; and it is not without its echoes within us ourselves (compare Matthew 13:7, 22). 'Blessed are the poor in spirit' (Matthew 5:3) – that points to the success of faith, as do all the beatitudes.

MOSES' PARENTS' FAITH

Hebrews **11:23**

[23] By faith Moses was hidden by his parents for three months after his birth, because they saw that the child was beautiful; and they were not afraid of the king's edict.

HIS parents did not know that the Lord meant their son Moses to become the leader of his people. Seeing 'that he was a fine baby' (Exodus 2:2; compare Acts 7:20), was what prompted them to hide him, and then put him under the protection of the king's daughter. How did that manifest faith? Keeping the child alive was more important for them than the king's threats. One can say that it was the Lord at work, without their knowing; it was the Lord who for his own purposes made the child's looks attractive and promising. Very well; but if so, faith can be at work in us by God's gift even when, for all we know, we are acting from ordinary motives.

Some people say they don't believe in God, and that they don't need God to live as humane and upright people; indeed, they say, some unbelievers live better lives than do some believers. It's an old point; but how do they know that God is not at work in them without their knowing? And maybe they are right not to believe in the 'God' they don't believe in!

Moses' parents and sister, yes, and Pharaoh's daughter too, plot to bring the child up alive rather than allow him to be killed. Their human response to a human baby is stronger than any respect for the inhumane decree of the king. A matter of natural instinct, one may say. Well, who planted that instinct in us? This baby is healthy and attractive, three months old and smiling or crying in his basket in the river, a presence that promises a future (as a leader or not). What about less fortunate babies? They too challenge the faith of their parents. None of them is just one of a number; each of them is like us all, uniquely loved by our Creator.

MOSES' FAITH (1)

Hebrews **11:24-26**

[24] By faith Moses, when he was grown up, refused to be called a son of Pharaoh's daughter, [25] choosing rather to share ill-treatment with the people of God than to enjoy the fleeting pleasures of sin. [26] He considered abuse suffered for the Christ to be greater wealth than the treasures of Egypt, for he was looking ahead to the reward.

BROUGHT up as a son of Pharaoh's daughter, living in the comfort of the royal court, Moses was suddenly taken back to where he came from. It started when he sided with the Hebrew and killed the Egyptian who was attacking him. That didn't oust him from his place as one of the top people until it became generally known; and even then, as he came to acknowledge his people, they were not yet ready to acknowledge him (Exodus 2:11-24). The story so far is very human, and shows that Moses himself is not really fit to lead the Lord's people until the Lord calls and sends him.

All the same, we are invited to see the grace and call of God already at work in him: 'by faith' it was that he turned his back on the privileges of the Egyptian court; 'by faith' (and prompted already by the Spirit) he chose 'rather to share ill-treatment with the people of God than to enjoy the fleeting pleasures of sin'. What sin could that have been? Spending his life 'at ease' in the Egyptian court (compare Amos 6:1-6), oblivious of the oppression it rested on.

Moses showed by his action that he sensed that; and we are invited to see his action as the start along a path of faith that would lead him beyond his present horizon. It would mean choosing to go for the as yet unseen future, considering 'abuse suffered for the Christ to be greater wealth than the treasures of Egypt' (compare Psalm 89:50-51). Although Moses did not yet know that this was God's people, he sensed the greatness that was to come (compare 1 Corinthians 2:9; Isaiah 64:4). And as he sided with the oppressed, he sided already with the Son (compare Matthew 25:31-46).

MOSES' FAITH (2)

Hebrews **11:27**

[27] By faith he left Egypt, unafraid of the king's anger; for he persevered as though he saw him who is invisible.

MOSES fled from Egypt because the king wanted to kill him (Exodus 2:15). None the less, we are prompted to see more in this than running away. Considering that Moses was the one God meant to use to save his people and to be a mediator on their behalf, we are to see here a tactical withdrawal into exile (Exodus 2:22), in which the Lord brings Moses to where he will tell him of his call (Exodus 3). The suggestion is that the gift of faith was at work in him within all his human motivation. He is said to have been in reality 'unafraid of the king's anger', and by the Lord's quiet guidance brought to a place from which to start and to which he was to return, 'the mountain of meeting'.

One of Moses' most famous traits is that the Lord would speak with him 'face to face, as one speaks to a friend' (Exodus 33:11), and that he was granted sight of the Lord's glory as far as one might see it and live. 'See, there is a place beside me where you shall stand on the rock; and while my glory passes by I will put you in a cleft of the rock, and I will cover you with my hand until I have passed by; then I will take away my hand, and you shall see my back; but my face shall not be seen' (Exodus 33:19-23; 34:4-8; compare Numbers 12:8).

That is the strength that was given to Moses throughout his career, to persevere as one who saw 'him who is invisible'. But this was still faith seeing in a glass darkly: 'you shall see my back'; *when you arrive where God is, you will find he has moved on* – until the Son comes to manifest him to all (1 Timothy 1:17; John 1:18).

MOSES' FAITH (3)

Hebrews **11:28**

[28] By faith he kept the Passover and the sprinkling of blood, so that the destroyer of the firstborn would not touch the firstborn of Israel.

WE may notice that the ritual in this connection is an expression of faith, a matter of fully accepting and doing what the Lord says is to be done for the salvation of his people (Exodus 12:8): 'by faith he kept the Passover and the sprinkling of blood, so that the destroyer of the firstborn would not touch the firstborn of Israel', so that he would *pass them by.*

The ten plagues (Exodus 7-12) are a competition between the Lord, working through Moses and Aaron, and the Egyptian magicians. By the third plague, the magicians admit that they cannot turn dust into gnats: 'This is the finger of God', they say (Exodus 8:19; compare Luke 11:20). By the end, the Egyptians beg the people to go away (Exodus 12:30-33).

So the people of Israel were protected from the plagues, and from Egyptian oppression. It was there and then that they were made people of the Lord; and the Pasch, the Passover, was to be an annual commemoration of that. True, the commemoration was forgotten for ages (2 Kings 23:22); it was taken up again to celebrate new signs of God's care for his people (see for example Ezra 6:19, 22). And this was itself a foreshadowing of the full renewal that was to come in the final proof of God's love, as 'our paschal lamb, Christ, has been sacrificed' – the punishment has passed by, sin has been overcome – 'therefore, let us celebrate the festival, not with the old yeast, the yeast of malice and evil, but with the unleavened bread of sincerity and truth' (1 Corinthians 5:7-8). And this Pasch is open to all who come to it in faith (contrast Exodus 12:43-49; and compare Romans 3:29-31).

THE PEOPLE'S FAITH (1)

Hebrews **11:29**

[29] By faith the people passed through the Red Sea as if it were dry land, but when the Egyptians attempted to do so they were drowned.

'BY Pi-hahiroth, in front of Baal-zephon' was where the Egyptians overtook the Israelites, camped there after escaping from Egypt (Exodus 14:2, 9; compare Numbers 33:7; Deuteronomy 8:2); and there Pharaoh thought he had them in a narrow place. The people too thought they were captured (compare Psalm 106:7-8), and Moses had to encourage them: 'Do not be afraid, stand firm, and see the deliverance that the Lord will accomplish for you today' (Exodus 14:10-14).

Although they had hesitated, it can truly be said that 'by faith the people passed through the Red Sea as if it were dry land', relying on the power of the Lord rather than on themselves. The suggestion is that the Egyptians relied on their own power; that that was their lack of faith, and their disaster.

The miracle became a powerful memory of God's love for his people: 'He rebuked the Red Sea, and it became dry; he led them through the deep as through a desert' (Psalm 106:9; compare 114:5); and it was used to kindle a hope that he would work wonders again on behalf of his people (compare Isaiah 43:16; 51:10). It continues to be a vivid image and a warning to the people of the New Covenant in Christ (1 Corinthians 10:1-13).

'Between Pi-hahiroth a Baal-zephon': there the people realise they are helpless in face of the enemy; and it is there that the Lord leads them to safety by a completely unexpected escape route. That, after all, is how faith works (compare 2 Corinthians 12:7-10), by opening up fully to God's grace. Through the sea of adversity God opens for us a way into his bliss.

THE PEOPLE'S FAITH (2)

Hebrews 11:30-31

[30] By faith the walls of Jericho fell after they had been encircled for seven days. [31] By faith Rahab the prostitute did not perish with those who were disobedient, because she had received the spies in peace.

THE fall of Jericho, to the north of the Dead Sea, opened up the people's way into the Promised Land; it fell, however, not by force of arms, but by a miracle. Once again the victory was won not by human resources but by the Lord, working indeed through human cooperation inspired by faith. Rahab played her part in that, 'by faith' again. How so, if James could ask as part of his argument, 'was not Rahab the prostitute also justified by works when she welcomed the messengers and sent them out by another road?' (James 2:25)? Well, what is said here does not contradict that: her action, 'receiving the spies in peace', is reckoned to be an act of faith. That is why she and her family were saved from the destruction of Jericho; but more than that, she and hers were from then forward counted among the Lord's people (Joshua 6:25).

Talking selectively like this of the people's faith and Rahab's faith, neither the author of *Hebrews* nor we are committed to agreeing with the destruction of Jericho and all its people. What we are doing is tracing examples of adherence to the Lord through all the circumstances of history and through the medium of the nation's legends of its past. We have in fact a better model.

When the people of a Samaritan village refused to receive Jesus because he was on his way to Jerusalem, James and John asked him, 'Lord, do you want us to command fire to come down from heaven and consume them?' His answer was to rebuke them. And 'they went on to another village.' Some copies of that account add that he said to them, 'You do not know what spirit you are of' (Luke 9:51-56; 19:10).

THE FAITH OF THE NATION'S HEROES

Hebrews 11:32-34

[32] And what more should I say? For time would fail me to tell of Gideon, Barak, Samson, Jephthah, of David and Samuel and the prophets – [33] who through faith conquered kingdoms, administered justice, obtained promises, shut the mouths of lions, [34] quenched raging fire, escaped the

edge of the sword, won strength out of weakness, became mighty in war, put foreign armies to flight.

HAVING recalled the faith of the pilgrim travellers towards the Promised Land, we turn now briefly to the achievements of the heroes of the time of the judges and the time of the kings and prophets, achievements accomplished by faith. These were successes in this world, but not on terms of this world: defeating kingdoms, in spite of having smaller military power against greater (Judges 4-5, 7-8, 11, 14-16); delivering justice as a good and wise leader (1 Samuel 12:4; 2 Samuel 8:15; 1 Kings 10:9); laying hold of the promises, tasting present grace and hope for a better yet fulfilment.

It was not by their own resources that Daniel survived the lion's den and the three young men lived in the fiery furnace; many a one escaped the edge of the sword or was given strength in weakness; and the victories that were won were not to be attributed to human power. They all knew that God was saving his people to inherit better things.

In all these achievements, for sure, human effort was called for. Yes, and successful people do tend to claim the praise for themselves; it's our victory, or indeed mine. 'Not to us, O Lord, not to us, but to your name give glory, for the sake of your steadfast love and your faithfulness' (Psalm 115:1; compare Ezekiel 36:22-23).

At the same time, there was a further test of faith. Idols are taunted with their inability to do anything (Psalm 115:4--18), but what about the times that the Lord delays, the times that his cause or his people's cause fails instead of succeeding? (Psalm 83).

THE FAITH OF HEROIC WOMEN

Hebrews **11:35**

[35] Women received their dead by resurrection. Others were tortured, refusing to accept release, in order to obtain a better resurrection.

'WOMEN received their dead by resurrection.' They received them when a prophet acted in the name of the Lord. In the case of the widow's son at Zarephath, and Elijah's restoring him to life (1 Kings 17:17-24), the widow comes to believe after having her son stored to her: 'Now I know that you are a man of God, and that the word of the Lord in your mouth is truth'. In the case of the Shunammite woman's son (2 Kings 4:17-37), her faith in Elisha as a man of God is there already at the start: 'I am sure that this man who regularly passes our way is a holy man of God' (4:9).

A similar difference can be found in the New Testament. In the story of raising Dorcas (Acts 9:36-41) faith comes to the neighbours as a result of the miracle: 'many believed in the Lord'. In the Lazarus case (John 11), both Martha and Mary (by her action) believe in Jesus already (21-22), and in the resurrection (23-24), and welcome Jesus' declaration that he is the resurrection and the life (25-26). Nothing is said about the response of the widowed mother of Nain (Luke 7:11-17), but that Jesus 'had compassion for her and said to her "do not weep" '. Anyhow, the New Testament too has women receiving their dead restored to life.

Faith is needed in the presence of the Lord of life and death. Lack of faith may obstruct his power. ' "The child is not dead, but sleeping", he said, and they laughed at him' (Mark 5:38-43); having already encouraged her father to believe (36), Jesus took her by the hand and called her back to wake up from the sleep of death. Straight afterwards, according to Mark (6:1-6), in Jesus' home town, 'he could do no deed of power there' because of their unbelief.

I believe; help my unbelief. (Mark 9:24).

95

FAITH IN ADVERSITY

Hebrews 11:35-38

[35] Women received their dead by resurrection. Others were tortured, refusing to accept release, in order to obtain a better resurrection. [36] Others suffered mocking and flogging, and even chains and imprisonment. [37] They were stoned to death, they were sawn in two, they were killed by the sword; they went about in skins of sheep and goats, destitute, persecuted, tormented – [38] of whom the world was not worthy. They wandered in deserts and mountains, and in caves and holes in the ground.

THE faithful will not win every contest, nor will they escape every time from pain and death. Faith has a better victory in view. In spite of suffering and death – and failure in the sight of the world – a living faith can ask in the teeth of death, 'where, O death, is your victory?' (1 Corinthians 15:54; compare Isaiah 25:8; Hosea 13:14; Hebrews 2:14-15).

In the second book of Maccabees, Eleazar refused the escape offered him (2 Maccabees 6:18-31), and the seven brothers (7:1-42) faced torture and death one after the other with loyal faith and hope, declaring 'the King of the universe will raise us up to an everlasting renewal of life, because we have died for his laws' (7:9; compare their mother's answer, 7:20-23, 29).

'Others', without dying, 'suffered mocking and flogging, and even chains and imprisonment' (1 Kings 22:26--27; Jeremiah 37:11-21; 1 Maccabees 13:12-24). It is not always easy to be a faithful witness to God's love (compare Matthew 5:11-12). That is how it was, and is, and shall be, in this world's view. And we can't expect to win every argument either.

Even without facing instant death, the Lord's witnesses found themselves going about without comfortable home or clothing (Matthew 11:8), people 'of whom the world was not worthy' wandering 'in deserts and mountains, and in caves and holes in the ground'. 'Blessed are the poor in spirit'! 'Foxes have holes, and birds of the air have nests, but the Son of Man has nowhere to lay his head' (Matthew 8:20; compare Matthew 6:19-21).

BRINGING ALL TO COMPLETION TOGETHER

Hebrews **11:39-40**

[39] Yet all these, though they were commended for their faith, did not receive what was promised, [40] since God had provided something better so that they would not, apart from us, be made perfect.

GOD did, of course, care for his faithful from age to age, and give them all his love ('Abraham rejoiced that he would see my day' – John 8:56). All the same, they did not personally experience the fulfilment of the promises. In God's plan, that was to include us, and to turn out better than every old desire, better than the promises promised. They died before seeing and hearing what we have been given to see and hear (compare Matthew 13:17; Luke 10:24; 1 Peter 1:10-12).

A large element in their faith was that they knew this, that 'a thousand years in your sight are like yesterday when it is past, or like a watch in the night' (Psalm 90:4; compare 2 Peter 3:8-9). 'The counsel of the Lord stands for ever, the thoughts of his heart to all generations' (Psalm 33:11).

God's purpose was to 'gather up all things' in Christ, 'things in heaven and things on earth' (Ephesians 1:9-10). 'In him all the fullness of God was pleased to dwell, and through him God was pleased to reconcile to himself all things, whether on earth or in heaven, by making peace through the blood of his cross' (Colossians 1:19-20; compare 2 Corinthians 5:18-19).

We have received this Gospel, as they did not in their time, but we have not yet reached the end of our journey. Jesus has opened the way into the sanctuary, and we can approach the throne of grace in him, but the plan has not yet been fulfilled in us (compare Philippians 3:12-14); it won't be finally fulfilled, until we, together with those of old, are brought to perfection in him in the glory. Our testing is not over yet (Hebrews 10:36-39), although they are already there in glory awaiting us.

Letter to the Hebrews

Chapter 12

[1] Therefore, since we are surrounded by so great a cloud of witnesses, let us also lay aside every weight and the sin that clings so closely, and let us run with perseverance the race that is set before us, [2] looking to Jesus the pioneer and perfecter of our faith, who for the sake of the joy that was set before him endured the cross, disregarding its shame, and has taken his seat at the right hand of the throne of God. [3] Consider him who endured such hostility against himself from sinners, so that you may not grow weary or lose heart. [4] In your struggle against sin you have not yet resisted to the point of shedding your blood. [5] And you have forgotten the exhortation that addresses you as children – 'My child, do not regard lightly the discipline of the Lord, or lose heart when you are punished by him; [6] for the Lord disciplines those whom he loves, and chastises every child whom he accepts.' [7] Endure trials for the sake of discipline. God is treating you as children; for what child is there whom a parent does not discipline? [8] If you do not have that discipline in which all children share, then you are illegitimate and not his children. [9] Moreover, we had human parents to discipline us, and we respected them. Should we not be even more willing to be subject to the Father of spirits and live? [10] For they disciplined us for a short time as seemed best to them, but he disciplines us for our good, in order that we may share his holiness. [11] Now, discipline always seems painful rather than pleasant at the time, but later it yields the peaceful fruit of righteousness to those who have been trained by it. [12] Therefore lift your drooping hands and strengthen your weak knees, [13] and make straight paths for your feet, so that what is lame may not be put out of joint,

but rather be healed. [14] Pursue peace with everyone, and the holiness without which no one will see the Lord. [15] See to it that no one fails to obtain the grace of God; that no root of bitterness springs up and causes trouble, and through it many become defiled. [16] See to it that no one becomes like Esau, an immoral and godless person, who sold his birthright for a single meal. [17] You know that later, when he wanted to inherit the blessing, he was rejected, for he found no chance to repent, even though he sought the blessing with tears. [18] You have not come to something that can be touched, a blazing fire, and darkness, and gloom, and a tempest, [19] and the sound of a trumpet, and a voice whose words made the hearers beg that not another word be spoken to them. [20] (For they could not endure the order that was given, 'If even an animal touches the mountain, it shall be stoned to death.' [21] Indeed, so terrifying was the sight that Moses said, 'I tremble with fear.') [22] But you have come to Mount Zion and to the city of the living God, the heavenly Jerusalem, and to innumerable angels in festal gathering, [23] and to the assembly of the firstborn who are enrolled in heaven, and to God the judge of all, and to the spirits of the righteous made perfect, [24] and to Jesus, the mediator of a new covenant, and to the sprinkled blood that speaks a better word than the blood of Abel. [25] See that you do not refuse the one who is speaking; for if they did not escape when they refused the one who warned them on earth, how much less will we escape if we reject the one who warns from heaven! [26] At that time his voice shook the earth; but now he has promised, 'Yet once more I will shake not only the earth but also the heaven.' [27] This phrase, 'Yet once more,' indicates the removal of what is shaken – that is, created things – so that what cannot be shaken may remain. [28] Therefore, since we are receiving a kingdom that cannot be shaken, let us give thanks, by which we offer to God an acceptable worship with reverence and awe; [29] for indeed our God is a consuming fire.

THE CLOUD OF WITNESSES

Hebrews **12:1**

[1] Therefore, since we are surrounded by so great a cloud of witnesses, let us also lay aside every weight and the sin that clings so closely, and let us run with perseverance the race that is set before us

THE scene changes: life is a career, a race (compare 1 Corinthians 9:24-26; 1 Timothy 6:12; 2 Timothy 4:7). We do not run in solitude, but in a stadium, as it were, where the spectators are the assembly of heaven, with 'a cloud of witnesses' about us, the crowd of those who have already borne witness to the Lord, our brothers and sisters whom the Lord has welcomed home already as his faithful witnesses.

To know they are watching us is a great encouragement, as we know they are on our side, and that they have run this race in their turn before us. By thinking of them we can discern the true meaning of our efforts, and see in them a guarantee that we too shall win through if we 'compete according to the rules' (compare 2 Timothy 2:5).

So it turns out that the previous chapter was not only a historical survey. Those who have been brought through the veil before us have indeed gone with Christ into the presence and the sight of eternal glory (compare John 8:56--58); but they are not, for all that, far away from us. Yes; we are still on this side of the veil, but we cannot avoid being in the presence of the unseen God who creates and supports us. We already live in Christ Jesus, and his Spirit already gives the beginnings of eternal life. In the grace of our Lord Jesus Christ and the love of God and the fellowship of the Holy Spirit we are not far from each other, on that side and on this.

Is that not true of our predecessors too, not only of the ancient Hebrews? Of those of our people, our family, our whole human race, all who have gone before us into the Presence, 'the dwelling place of God'? (Ephesians 2:14-22).

THE GREATEST EXAMPLE OF ALL

Hebrews 12:1-3

[1] Therefore, since we are surrounded by so great a cloud of witnesses, let us also lay aside every weight and the sin that clings so closely, and let us run with perseverance the race that is set before us, [2] looking to Jesus the pioneer and perfecter of our faith, who for the sake of the joy that was set before him endured the cross, disregarding its shame, and has taken his seat at the right hand of the throne of God. [3] Consider him who endured such hostility against himself from sinners, so that you may not grow weary or lose heart.

SURROUNDED by so great and friendly an audience, we are to 'lay aside every weight' of worldly concerns that can slow our progress (compare Luke 8:14-15; Matthew 6:31--33), 'and the sin that clings so closely', so as to 'run with perseverance the race that is set before us'. It is not, however, the support of that audience that will give us victory, neither is it our own self-discipline; faith is the key. In ordinary sports and athletics, people say, one needs a 'killer instinct', a readiness to commit all one's resources to the task. The key to this contest is to look to Jesus: in him above all we see the faith that was shown by those of old brought to its highest peak, the faith that we are to emulate. Jesus, in his humanity, became 'the pioneer and perfecter' of the faith of all the faithful, being as he is the chief and fullest exemplar of the self-giving that faith demands.

'In the days of his flesh' he went through the crisis of faith and obedience as one who saw the invisible (Hebrews 5:7-9; 11:27). 'For the sake of the joy that was set before him' (compare 2:9; Isaiah 53:10-11; John 15:11) as the goal of the race 'he endured the cross' without faltering, as we are asked to do, 'disregarding its shame' (don't let's forget how shameful it was). Consequently, Jesus 'has taken his seat at the right hand of the throne of God' (compare 1:3; 8:1; 10:12; Philippians 2:9-11).

His is no example offered from far off; Jesus is near us (2:17-18), allowing us to share both his sufferings and his glory (Philippians 3:10-11; 1 Peter 4:13; 2 Corinthians 1:3-7).

THE LORD'S DISCIPLINE

Hebrews **12:3-6**

[3] Consider him who endured such hostility against himself from sinners, so that you may not grow weary or lose heart. [4] In your struggle against sin you have not yet resisted to the point of shedding your blood. [5] And you have forgotten the exhortation that addresses you as children – 'My child, do not regard lightly the discipline of the Lord, or lose heart when you are punished by him; [6] for the Lord disciplines those whom he loves, and chastises every child whom he accepts.'

OTHER people have sealed their witness with their blood, against injustice and untruth unto death, some of them long ago and some in our time; and Jesus is both leader and brother to them in this too, 'to the point of death'.

The Hebrews, on the other hand 'have not yet resisted to the point of shedding (their) blood' in their 'struggle against sin' (and neither have we!); they wince under afflictions that are much less, having 'forgotten the exhortation' that explains such experiences as the discipline a father gives his children out of love for them, and because he acknowledges them as his own children (compare 1 Corinthians 11:32; Deuteronomy 8:2-5).

The old Lenten practice was to eat less, to fast, and to give to the needy – two things that have not died out in our own time; still, the central purpose was and is to prepare for Easter by practising the discipline that is part of the life of faith (compare 1 Corinthians 9:24-27), to wean us from the excessive attractions of this world (compare Matthew 13:22), to strengthen our conversion from sin, and to kindle in us more effective love for God and our neighbour.

Active discipline of that sort may well be beneficial to us all; it is certainly necessary for turning away from sin. Anyhow we might remember that there is a self-discipline in face of the small annoyances of life, and a putting-up with people whose ways do not suit us. We can benefit from unpleasant experiences of this sort by using them to bring us nearer to the One who loves both them and us, and who puts up with us.

DISCIPLINED BY OUR FATHER?

Hebrews **12:7-8**

[7] Endure trials for the sake of discipline. God is treating you as children; for what child is there whom a parent does not discipline? [8] If you do not have that discipline in which all children share, then you are illegitimate and not his children.

THIS image has another side to it. We are sometimes tempted to blame God for what happens to us: how could a truly loving father treat his child in this way? Or even allow this or that to happen if he could prevent it? We have to remember that this is an image, a picture, a parable, and that no comparison can ever be complete. God's love is fuller and more far-reaching than any of our pictures of it could convey; his wonders are ample enough to wake us up and surprise us throughout eternity (compare 1 Corinthians 2:9). Anyhow, it is better to complain to him rather than about him.

To think about God, we need a multiplicity of images and ideas that will correct each other as each of them falls short of representing him. And certainly we don't have to think that everything that is done by the powers and circumstances and people of the world is an 'act of God'. Calling

God 'Father' is a picture in a parable too. God is surely better than any human father, or indeed mother.

Still, this is the parable used here: God as a father disciplining his children, and in that very act recognizing them as his children, as we noted already: 'Endure trials for the sake of discipline. God is treating you as children.' In the parable, it is as though our trials are sent us direct from God, for our good. Chrysostom informs us, 'If you had no affliction, then you would have to think that God had deserted you, rather than when you were afflicted'. Gerard Manley Hopkins expressed the same truth: 'I feel thy finger and find thee'.

We might suppose that this is all very well in terms of the parable. However, the experience of the ages seems to suggest that God's friends get it hardest. 'That's why you have so few of them', Teresa of Jesus reportedly said to God once. But all the same their hardship does not exactly come from God.

THE HEAVENLY DISCIPLINE (1)

Hebrews 12:9-11

[9] Moreover, we had human parents to discipline us, and we respected them. Should we not be even more willing to be subject to the Father of spirits and live? [10] For they disciplined us for a short time as seemed best to them, but he disciplines us for our good, in order that we may share his holiness. [11] Now, discipline always seems painful rather than pleasant at the time, but later it yields the peaceful fruit of righteousness to those who have been trained by it.

'ONE of the final stages in one's growing up is when one becomes able at last to forgive one's parents!' it has been said. 'To forgive them for what?' 'For being one's parents.' 'Why for that?' 'Because parents are a dominant presence (or sometimes absence) in a child's life, to a degree that can seem oppressive. They were bigger than us and stronger; they were already there before us. Up-bringing can be stifling, sometimes.' True enough, wise up-bringing will give the child room to develop his or her own personality and identity. The wise parents will say to the child, 'At first you'll do what is right because we tell you; but you will have to grow into doing what is right because you see it to be right.' Such an up-bringing will foster mutual respect between parents and child.

Against a family background like that we have a chance to develop an appreciation of God's fatherhood. On that pattern, 'We had human parents to discipline us, and we respected them.' But even so, our relationship with God is deeper in every way. We cannot ever grow into equality with God so as to be independent of him; and on the other hand the freedom and room to live that God gives us is far beyond what human resources could ever give. 'Should we not be even more willing to be subject to the Father of spirits and live?'

One phase of forgiving our parents is when we realise at last that they were just as fallible as us. 'They disciplined us… as seemed best to them'; but God knows what will truly be for our good. How could we ever have something to forgive him?

THE HEAVENLY DISCIPLINE (2)

Hebrews 12:12-13

[12] Therefore lift your drooping hands and strengthen your weak knees, [13] and make straight paths for your feet, so that what is lame may not be put out of joint, but rather be healed.

WHEN we are disappointed, hurt, crossed, unfairly treated, whether as disciples or as ourselves (compare 2 Corinthians 11:23-29), we can and we should accept that as discipline.

106

We do not suppose that the Lord does these things to us, but we recognize that this is an unavoidable part of being his disciples (compare Matthew 5:11-12). Ignatius of Antioch implored: 'Pray for me to have strength within and without to be a Christian not in name only but in truth… I shall then be a true disciple of Jesus Christ, when my body is no longer in sight of the world… now I am beginning to be a disciple.' (Ignatius of Antioch, *Romans*, III-V).

We need the painful discipline, at very least a frequent light touch of it, to train us not to rely too much on this world's possessions and advantages, however good they are, and indeed because they can be very good. To have my own way, to stand on my own feet, that's very good; but to make that the basis of my security will make me lose sight of obedience to the Word of God (Philippians 2:1-8), and of my status as a pilgrim to a better land. Possessions too are hard to do without; but to be a disciple one needs to aim beyond the security that they can seem to give (Luke 12:22--34). Family too, which one may think is the best support we can have on earth, can be an obstacle to discipleship if one rests in it too contentedly (Matthew 10:34-39).

When we meet disappointment in any of these good things, let us accept it as a prompting to turn nearer to where we should be; and to turn to the One with whom our affliction makes us one (Colossians 1:24).

LET US NOT REFUSE GOD'S GRACE

Hebrews 12:14-17

[14] Pursue peace with everyone, and the holiness without which no one will see the Lord. [15] See to it that no one fails to obtain the grace of God; that no root of bitterness springs up and causes trouble, and through it many become defiled. [16] See to it that no one becomes like Esau, an immoral and godless person, who sold his birthright for a single meal. [17] You know that later, when he wanted to inherit the blessing,

he was rejected, for he found no chance to repent, even though he sought the blessing with tears.

TO live as faithful disciples means pursuing peace with everyone, and giving oneself to the life of 'holiness without which no one will see the Lord' (Matthew 5:8-9; Psalm 34:14; Romans 12:18; 1 Corinthians 13:12; Luke 21:34-35).

As disciples of Jesus the audience of the *Letter* are a community – the people of the new covenant – meant to care for each other, and to 'see to it', as far as may be, 'that no one fails to obtain the grace of God; that no root of bitterness springs up and causes trouble' (no such man either; compare Acts 8:23), causing many to become defiled (compare Deuteronomy 29:18-19). 'See to it that no one becomes like Esau, an immoral and godless person, who sold his birthright for a single meal', so turning his back on God's blessings, refusing the call to faith. He lost his birthright because the decision to bless his brother was final; but he was not sent away without any blessing (Genesis 27:39; 33:1-17).

Here again we have the old language and examples, but with the significance of the new covenant: peace with everyone, living as people who are being drawn nearer to God in Christ, a new people who together are to avoid falling away from the grace of God that is offered us in Christ Jesus. Now the Hebrew Christians would be behaving like Esau if they turned back from their Christian birthright to the familiar comforts of the earthly Temple. Is there an application to me, to us? We too are to promote true peace and grow nearer to God in Christ, are we not? (Philippians 3:12-21).

NOT SINAI BUT ZION

Hebrews **12:18-24**

[18] You have not come to something that can be touched, a blazing fire, and darkness, and gloom, and a tempest, [19] and the sound of a trumpet, and a voice whose words made the hearers beg that not another word be spoken to them. [20] (For they could not endure the order that was given, 'If even an animal touches the mountain, it shall be stoned to death.' [21] Indeed, so terrifying was the sight that Moses said, 'I tremble with fear.') [22] But you have come to Mount Zion and to the city of the living God, the heavenly Jerusalem, and to innumerable angels in festal gathering, [23] and to the assembly of the firstborn who are enrolled in heaven, and to God the judge of all, and to the spirits of the righteous made perfect, [24] and to Jesus, the mediator of a new covenant, and to the sprinkled blood that speaks a better word than the blood of Abel.

'IN many and various ways', indeed. Here comes the majestic finale of the symphony (though there is still a coda to follow). Awe, and indeed terror, was the effect when the Lord spoke to the whole people from Mount Sinai, the earthly mountain, to proclaim the first covenant (Exodus 19:12-25; 20:18-20; Deuteronomy 4:11-12). Even Moses trembled with fear.

The new covenant, however, is marked by grace and joy and glory: 'you have come to Mount Zion and to the city of the living God, the heavenly Jerusalem' (compare John 4:21-24; Revelation 21:2); not to some mountain in the wilderness, but to the home of the living God, to the home of his family. The picture reminds us of the book of Revelation: 'to innumerable angels in festal gathering' (compare Revelation 5:11), 'and to the assembly of the firstborn who are enrolled in heaven (compare Luke 10:20; Revelation 3:5; Exodus 32:32-33; Isaiah 4:3; Malachi 3:16). Who are this 'assembly', this *ecclesia*? Who else but the children of

God by adoption, the citizens of heaven, into whose company we are offered access in Christ? 'There the joy of each will be multiplied by joy for the joy of every other taken as one's own' (Thomas Aquinas).

God is at the heart of all this, God and his rightful judgement; the old faithful witnesses are with him in Christ; and there on his right hand is our brother Jesus, the mediator of the new covenant which he has sealed with his own human blood.

A CONSUMING FIRE!

Hebrews 12:25-29

[25] See that you do not refuse the one who is speaking; for if they did not escape when they refused the one who warned them on earth, how much less will we escape if we reject the one who warns from heaven! [26] At that time his voice shook the earth; but now he has promised, 'Yet once more I will shake not only the earth but also the heaven.' [27] This phrase, 'Yet once more,' indicates the removal of what is shaken – that is, created things – so that what cannot be shaken may remain. [28] Therefore, since we are receiving a kingdom that cannot be shaken, let us give thanks, by which we offer to God an acceptable worship with reverence and awe; [29] for indeed our God is a consuming fire.

THE Lord who speaks to us in his Son is the same Lord who spoke to the people of old from Sinai. He does not threaten us; the threat arises from the very nature of things. 'If we reject the one who warns from heaven' we are not faced with a risk of external loss and punishment so much as a risk of losing the only hope there is of having true life.

All created things will come to an end, leaving only 'what cannot be shaken'; to those things we should cling, the things of 'the kingdom that cannot be shaken'.

We are not to fear that God will punish us (although that is how the thing is expressed: Hebrews 10:31); rather, that we may lose him by our lack of loyalty, of faith and love (Hebrews 4:11-13). That is how we are to take the saying that 'our God is a consuming fire' (Deuteronomy 4:24; 9:3); there is in the Bible a development of understanding God's justice, faithfulness and loving kindness. Our God is indeed the same Lord; but the Gospel amplifies our discernment of who he is.

The fire will indeed consume the dross of sin (Malachi 3:2-12; Isaiah 33:14-16; 1 Corinthians 3:10-17). God, who is love through and through, cannot be angry. To refuse God is to refuse love; and when one refuses God or refuses love, it is that refusal that turns the offer into an experience of anger. One finds that 'God's anger' in one's own refusal of him. That is what hell must be. God's righteousness is mercy; and turning away from that is what makes it into punishment and anger for the one who turns away (Romans 1:16-32).

So 'let us give thanks, by which we offer to God an acceptable worship with reverence and awe'; yes, and with love.

Letter to the Hebrews

Chapter 13

[1] Let mutual love continue. [2] Do not neglect to show hospitality to strangers, for by doing that some have entertained angels without knowing it. [3] Remember those who are in prison, as though you were in prison with them; those who are being tortured, as though you yourselves were being tortured. [4] Let marriage be held in honour by all, and let the marriage bed be kept undefiled; for God will judge fornicators and adulterers. [5] Keep your lives free from the love of money, and be content with what you have; for he has said, 'I will never leave you or forsake you.' [6] So we can say with confidence, 'The Lord is my helper; I will not be afraid. What can anyone do to me?' [7] Remember your leaders, those who spoke the word of God to you; consider the outcome of their way of life, and imitate their faith. [8] Jesus Christ is the same yesterday and today and forever. [9] Do not be carried away by all kinds of strange teachings; for it is well for the heart to be strengthened by grace, not by regulations about food, which have not benefited those who observe them. [10] We have an altar from which those who officiate in the tent have no right to eat. [11] For the bodies of those animals whose blood is brought into the sanctuary by the high priest as a sacrifice for sin are burned outside the camp. [12] Therefore Jesus also suffered outside the city gate in order to sanctify the people by his own blood. [13] Let us then go to him outside the camp and bear the abuse he endured. [14] For here we have no lasting city, but we are looking for the city that is to come. [15] Through him, then, let us continually offer a sacrifice of praise to God, that is, the fruit of lips that confess his name. [16] Do not neglect to do good and to share what you have, for such sacrifices are pleasing to God. [17] Obey

your leaders and submit to them, for they are keeping watch over your souls and will give an account. Let them do this with joy and not with sighing – for that would be harmful to you. [18] Pray for us; we are sure that we have a clear conscience, desiring to act honourably in all things. [19] I urge you all the more to do this, so that I may be restored to you very soon. [20] Now may the God of peace, who brought back from the dead our Lord Jesus, the great shepherd of the sheep, by the blood of the eternal covenant, [21] make you complete in everything good so that you may do his will, working among us that which is pleasing in his sight, through Jesus Christ, to whom be the glory forever and ever. Amen. [22] I appeal to you, brothers and sisters, bear with my word of exhortation, for I have written to you briefly. [23] I want you to know that our brother Timothy has been set free; and if he comes in time, he will be with me when I see you. [24] Greet all your leaders and all the saints. Those from Italy send you greetings. [25] Grace be with all of you.

RIGHT LIVING

Hebrews **13:1-6**

[1] Let mutual love continue. [2] Do not neglect to show hospitality to strangers, for by doing that some have entertained angels without knowing it. [3] Remember those who are in prison, as though you were in prison with them; those who are being tortured, as though you yourselves were being tortured. [4] Let marriage be held in honour by all, and let the marriage bed be kept undefiled; for God will judge fornicators and adulterers. [5] Keep your lives free from the love of money, and be content with what you have; for he has said, 'I will never leave you or forsake you.' [6] So we can say with confidence, 'The Lord is my helper; I will not be afraid. What can anyone do to me?'

AS people of the new covenant, we have a new inspiration to live well, as would be expected of good human beings anyway. 'Let mutual love continue' – continue, notice, as desirable as ever (Psalm 133; Deuteronomy 23:19), between disciples (John 13:35; Romans 12:10).

Even in time of trouble and persecution we ought not to neglect hospitality, because it has enabled some to entertain 'angels without knowing it' (Genesis 18-19; Tobit 5-7; Luke 10:34-35; 11:5-8; 14:12-14). The point of that advice was remembered by some even in prison camps. We are encouraged to remember some who do not ask for help but need it, 'those who are in prison, as though you were in prison with them; those who are being tortured, as though you yourselves were being tortured' (2 Corinthians 11:29) – and there is unfortunately nothing out of date about this.

It's worth remarking that talk of morals doesn't immediately mean sex, as it is often taken to do nowadays; all the same, chastity and faithfulness in marriage are an important part of Christian living (Ephesians 5:5, 21-33). 'God will judge fornicators and adulterers': why? Surely because they treat other people as means for their own satisfaction; and because God's love is the basis of the dignity of every one of his people, and the basis of every equal and healthy relationship between his people (1 Thessalonians 4:3-9; compare Tobit 7-8).

'The love of money is a root of all kinds of evil' (1 Timothy 6:3-10). 'Be content with what you have': without every trying or wishing to win the lottery?

REMEMBER YOUR LEADERS

Hebrews 13:7

[7]Remember your leaders, those who spoke the word of God to you; consider the outcome of their way of life, and imitate their faith.

THE memory of the heroes of old is shared by all Jews; the Christian 'Hebrews' have special memories of the first leaders of their community, 'those who spoke the word of God to you' (compare 2:3; Luke 22:26; Acts 15:22; 1 Timothy 5:17; Acts 8:25). They did not merely speak; their way of life bore witness, as did their suffering, persecution, and their faithfulness to the end (Wisdom of Solomon 2:12-20). Remembering them is not enough. We should consider how to imitate them in our lives, as they imitated Christ (1 Corinthians 11:1).

We are to 'imitate their faith' rather than copy exactly what the first leaders of the community did in their time and place. When Chrysostom says 'It was their faith that settled them in the way they were to follow; their ways would not have been holy if they had hesitated in face of what was to come', he refers to their own circumstances: 'The way that they were to follow'. We are to imitate them by going forward in the manner we are uniquely called to, in our own circumstances; this calls for both faith and discernment. What is to be common to us and them is the spirit, the mind, the self-giving that keeps its sights on the 'pioneer and perfecter of our faith' (12:2).

Francis of Assisi, Teresa of Jesus, Maximilian Kolbe, John Vianney – pick your own examples – what is common to them all is faith and hope and love, that they imitated Jesus Christ our Lord, and that they are examples of his grace at work in people, nourishing each one to be a unique mirror of his glory (Revelation 2:17; 14:1; 22:4). May it work in us!

JESUS CHRIST

Hebrews **13:8**

[8] Jesus Christ is the same yesterday and today and forever.

'JESUS Christ is the same yesterday today and for ever.' He was with them, is with you, and will be with those who

115

will be, until the end of the world. The 'yesterday' here refers immediately to the leaders who have gone, but rings true with a wider reference for us.

Lord Jesus, you are the one for me, not because I have chosen you, but because you have loved me and given yourself for me. You have searched me and known me; under the fig tree, before I came to you, you saw me. I have no fear, because you are the first and the last and the living One; you died, and are alive for ever and ever, holding the keys of death and the dwelling-place of the dead; you have the words of eternal life.

To cling to any other as I want to cling to you would be captivity. To be your captive is to be free, because you are you. You are a finite man, human as we are, born of a woman; you experienced tiredness and hunger and thirst, yes, and death on the cross. But you are also the Son whom God 'appointed heir of all things, through whom he also created the worlds' (Hebrews 1:2); you are the Word who was in the beginning, the way, the truth and the life. Without you there is no going; with you to bring us we go through to the Father. Without you there is no knowing the truth; in you we can know you and your Father. Without you life is death; in you we are enabled to live more fully than anyone could imagine.

Good master, good Jesus, let me never separate myself from you. Never let me close my mind and heart to the greatness of your love.

THE SENSE OF THE FAITH

Hebrews **13:9**

[9] Do not be carried away by all kinds of strange teachings; for it is well for the heart to be strengthened by grace, not by regulations about food, which have not benefited those who observe them.

THE warning here is against any teaching whose practical result is to turn people away from allegiance to Jesus Christ. To belong to him, to put our faith in him, means acknowledging the truth about him; that is a matter of teaching, to be sure, with all its implications (compare Galatians 1:6-9); and *Hebrews* is an eloquent presentation of that teaching. We are to centre, however, on the One the teachings are about.

The heart of faith is on this side of every expression of it, and the best expression of doctrine always falls short. 'One Lord, one faith, one baptism, one God and Father of all, who is above all and through all and in all', who has revealed himself to us in his Son: that is doctrine, indeed, and what it says is true about the love that is beyond all saying (compare 1 Corinthians 8:1; 1 John 2:20). 'The evangelist John had only human words to express the mystery which is beyond expression; he learnt the mystery there where he laid his head at the Supper, and there we are to learn it in our turn' (Augustine).

We must not be carried away by 'strange teachings', various and curious and capricious, thought up by people's trickery, by their craftiness in deceitful scheming. Instead, we must speak and follow 'the truth in love, we must grow up in every way into him who is the head, into Christ' (Ephesians 4:14-15). And this itself is not a matter of using correct teachings to knock incorrect teachings on the head; how do we know that our own discernment is completely correct? No – we are to seek our roots in Christ Jesus, and in him in the fullness of God (Colossians 1:19-20; 2:6-7), until his Spirit becomes in us, as it were, an instinct to recognize the truth (compare 1 John 2:20, 26-27).

OUR ALTAR

Hebrews **13:9-10**

[9] Do not be carried away by all kinds of strange teachings; for it is well for the heart to be strengthened by grace, not by regulations about food, which have not benefited those who observe them. [10] We have an altar from which those who officiate in the tent have no right to eat.

YES, the *Hebrews*-author says; we have a better altar, and a more excellent heavenly food. We have no need to feel deprived at no longer sharing in the earthly tent of meeting. Those who officiate in that tent, that tabernacle of the old covenant, have no right to share our sacrificial meal. Already in the first century this was plain: 'No one is to eat or drink of your Eucharist, other than those who have been baptized in the name of the Lord' (Didache 9:5).

For the Christian, there is only one sacrifice, namely Jesus, and one altar, namely the Cross. 'This altar', says St. Thomas, 'is either the Cross of Christ on which he was sacrificed, or else Christ himself, in whom and through whom we offer our prayers; and that is what the 'golden altar' stands for' (compare Revelation 8:3).

Perhaps the reference here is not directly to the Eucharist, but don't let us forget the way belief in Jesus, the bread of life, develops in the synagogue at Capernaum to mean 'eat my flesh and drink my blood', since 'the bread that I will give is my flesh, for the life of the world' (John 6:29-33, 51-58). 'The cup of the Lord', 'the table of the Lord' (1 Corinthians 10:21) commemorate the one sacrifice, enabling the faithful in a mysterious and wonderful way to share in it (1 Corinthians 11:23-26; compare John 6:56-58 again).

He was crucified outside the camp to set a new sacrifice on a new altar; so that the cross of Christ should be an altar not only in the Temple, but also outside in the whole world. (Leo the Great).

LET US GO TO HIM

Hebrews **13:11-13**

[11] For the bodies of those animals whose blood is brought into the sanctuary by the high priest as a sacrifice for sin are burned outside the camp. [12] Therefore Jesus also suffered outside the city gate in order to sanctify the people by his own blood. [13] Let us then go to him outside the camp and bear the abuse he endured.

INDEED, the altar ministers of the old tabernacle could not eat from that altar either (because the offering was wholly consumed by fire: Leviticus 4:7-21; 6:23; 16:27; compare Ezekiel 44:10-14). So we have a privilege which doubly and more surpasses theirs: the sacrifice in which we share is inexpressibly more effective, and our sharing in it a spiritual fulfilment.

'The bodies of those animals whose blood is brought into the sanctuary by the high priest as a sacrifice for sin are burned outside the camp'. Jesus too 'suffered outside the city gate in order to sanctify the people by his own blood' (compare 9:12; John 19:17-20; Acts 7:58). Jesus did this 'to sanctify the people' (10:10), yes; by making a new covenant in his blood (compare 10:29; Luke 22:20), to make us God's people, and more than that, to make us his sons and daughters (compare 2:13).

It was by faith that Abraham left his own country, and by faith that these Hebrews leave their old community. From the point of view of earthly sight and experience, this is like going out of the camp with the scapegoat, maybe under abuse and curse, since they are going to him 'outside the camp' to 'bear the abuse he endured'; and that is a privilege to the eyes of faith (compare Luke 9:23-24). From the point of view of believing without seeing, this 'going out' means going with Jesus into the heavenly sanctuary; faith and hope and love are needed to keep hold of what is true before the Lord (Romans 8:18-25). We need faith in the Son who was 'burnt without being consumed' (2 Timothy 2:11-13; Exodus 3:2-3).

119

TOWARDS THE HEAVENLY CITY

Hebrews **13:14-16**

[14] For here we have no lasting city, but we are looking for the city that is to come. [15] Through him, then, let us continually offer a sacrifice of praise to God, that is, the fruit of lips that confess his name. [16] Do not neglect to do good and to share what you have, for such sacrifices are pleasing to God.

LOSING the earthly Jerusalem and its seeming safety can mean being scattered all over the world, as much 'strangers and pilgrims' as those of old; and certainly we should not yearn for what has been (compare 11:13-16). 'For here we have no lasting city, but we are looking for the city that is to come.' We are not ignorant of what city that is; our earthly pilgrimage is a journey towards it, and it is already in sight for the eye of faith (compare 12:22-24).

We note that it is through Jesus that the Hebrew Christians are exhorted to continually offer a sacrifice of praise to God. Jesus it is who has made us 'a kingdom, priests serving his God and Father' (Revelation 1:6), to offer 'a sacrifice of thanksgiving' (Psalm 50:14, 23), a sacrifice that will be fully acceptable in him and with him and through him, a Eucharist indeed.

We thank you, holy Father, for your holy name, given by you to dwell in our hearts, and for the knowledge and the faith and the immortality you have revealed to us through Jesus your Son; to you belongs the glory for ever and ever. (*Didache* 10:2).

The name of God is everything that manifests him. It is 'I AM', since he is the giver of being, the Creator (Exodus 3:14; Psalm 19:1). It is 'Jesus', because he is known in and by Jesus (John 14:9); we ourselves are his name, because the world's opinions about God often turn on what is seen in us (for better or for worse). 'Lips that confess his name' are not enough (Matthew 7:21-27); that is why they (and we) are warned not to 'neglect to do good and to share what you have, for such sacrifices are pleasing to God', and glorify his name.

AUTHORITY AND OBEDIENCE

Hebrews **13:17**

[17] Obey your leaders and submit to them, for they are keeping watch over your souls and will give an account. Let them do this with joy and not with sighing – for that would be harmful to you.

AS they were exhorted to consider the example of their former leaders, now the Hebrew Chrisitans are exhorted to obey the present leaders, who are 'keeping watch over your souls and will give an account'. As soon as there began to be leaders in the local churches, similar exhortations were given (1 Thessalonians 5:12-13). Yes; and if the members are asked to obey, the leaders are asked in their turn to be watchful, but doing that 'with joy and not with sighing' when they see their people growing and bearing fruit in the word of God. 'Souls' are the key, personal obedience to God and care for persons to prosper together before God.

What should one do if one's carefully formed conscientious judgement is that one ought not to obey the orders of one's spiritual leader? Some people held that even in such a case one ought to obey the leader as representing God. St Thomas Aquinas answered that that was mistaken: one's carefully formed conscientious judgement is in truth God's most immediate representative – going against that would be going against God. That does not do away with the authority of spiritual leaders; on the contrary, it explains it. Our usual obedience is for conscience's sake, because our considered judgement is that we should obey.

Well then, how should leaders carry on, with what attitude? That's the other side of the coin. 'Whoever wishes to be first among you must be slave of all' (Mark 10:35-45); 'washing feet' is their proper work (John 13:1-20), and teaching by example (1 Timothy 3:1-7).

ASKING FOR PRAYERS

Hebrews **13:18**

[18] Pray for us; we are sure that we have a clear conscience, desiring to act honourably in all things.

THE author himself doesn't address his audience from some unreachable height, as though he was quite safe from the dangers he is warning them against. If Jesus was tempted and trained by trials in the course of his life on earth, how much more will we all need prayers (preachers too, especially!) to keep us faithful and to support us in the Lord's work (1 Corinthians 9:27; Romans 15:30). 'Pray for us', he says.

In truth, 'we are sure that we have a clear conscience' (compare Acts 23:1; 2 Corinthians 1:12; 1 Timothy 3:9), 'desiring' as we do 'to act honourably in all things'. If one can say that, hand on heart, one still needs prayers. One may have done one's best to consider and act according to the light one has, and still make mistakes. We need to be and to act rightly, and not merely to think we do. (And some of you may think we are not right, not 'in all things', at least). Besides, the request for prayer is warmly personal, 'so that I may be restored to you very soon.'

Let us pray for our leaders in Church and state, for those who rule the countries of the world, for those who are in need and under foot; that is not in vain in Christ Jesus (1 Timothy 2:1-6). Let us ask God to guide the heads and hearts of those who seek justice by force of arms, so that they may act truly aright in all things; let us pray that his grace may reach what we think are the most inaccessible places, the people in whom we can see no good; and that his grace may have its way in us.

BLESSING AND GREETINGS
AND FAREWELL

Hebrews **13:20-25**

[20] Now may the God of peace, who brought back from the dead our Lord Jesus, the great shepherd of the sheep, by the blood of the eternal covenant, [21] make you complete in everything good so that you may do his will, working among us that which is pleasing in his sight, through Jesus Christ, to whom be the glory forever and ever. Amen. [22] I appeal to you, brothers and sisters, bear with my word of exhortation, for I have written to you briefly. [23] I want you to know that our brother Timothy has been set free; and if he comes in time, he will be with me when I see you. [24] Greet all your leaders and all the saints. Those from Italy send you greetings. [25] Grace be with all of you.

'NOW' the *Hebrews*-author expresses his prayer for his readers and listeners: 'may the God of peace' – they need peace in their trials and disputes – 'who brought back from the dead our Lord Jesus' (compare Romans 10:9) – defeating sin and death – 'the great shepherd of the sheep' (compare Isaiah 63:11), 'by the blood of the eternal covenant' (compare Zechariah 9:11), 'make you complete in everything good', equip you with his grace to 'do his will'; and may God work among us 'that which is pleasing in his sight, through Jesus Christ' – the Mediator in this too – 'to whom be the glory for ever and ever. Amen.'

You see how he shows virtue proceeding aright not entirely from God's action nor from our action alone (Chrysostom). *Believe that it all depends on God's grace, which it does;*

act, however, as though it all depends on your action, which it does.

The author of the *Letter* asks God to make the Hebrew Chrisitans responsible, fit to live well in every way; it is they who are to live, using their human capacities and opportunities (compare 1 Corinthians 15:8). Living by the Gospel is based on how any human being should live, although the challenge does not stop there (Mark 10:17-22). *Grace heals and develops nature.* So God offers one the grace to grow into the character and wisdom needed to live humanly well; and it is proper to ask God to shape, to work, to make among us (like a poet or a potter) 'that which is pleasing in his sight, through Jesus Christ', 'who will transform our humble body so that it may be conformed to the body of his glory' (Philippians 3:21).

LIVING IN FAITH TODAY (1)

Hebrews (all)

IN our world, the old temptations against faith are alive and well. Visible and tangible things are, if anything, more pressing, and the riches and powers of this world (or at least worry about them and desire for them) draw everyone's attention. 'How is your sex life?' ask the media persistently and in many ways; and the pervasive influence of the media seems to foster every other sort of greed and envy as well. 'The medium is the message', making the public image important, making the superficial crucial, and dismissing any unobvious truth.

Our life goes on in the midst of this. That is why people can think it easy to live without faith in God, and all the same to live as decent and normal people. And indeed there are many people who live tidily and humanely without much indication that religion counts for anything with them; while on the other hand there are religious people whose lives are in various ways far from being tidy and humane.

It is not clear that 'unreligious' good people do not in reality 'walk with God', and that by faith that they do not recognize as such; we can thank God for leading each and everyone in his own secret way; nor is it obvious either how far faith is effectively present in 'religious' people who go astray. It is not ours to judge, as we have been told (Matthew 7:1-5; compare 1 Kings 19:18). But 'hallowed be thy name', in us too.

'The trouble is that good people get weary' (Pius XII). We know to whom to turn when we are weary and heavy--burdened (Matthew 11:28-30).

LIVING IN FAITH TODAY (2)

Hebrews (all)

THE old monk (Dom Illtyd Trethowan) had thought and taught and written a great deal during his long life about how God is to be known in this world, and about the difficulties of the unbeliever. At the last philosophy conference that he attended, when he was over eighty years of age, the discussion was concerned again with the old question, how to prove the existence of God, and can it be proved. When he found a gap in the discussion, he just said 'I know he exists'.

That no doubt was a declaration of faith, but it was also a philosophical statement. The appeal to one's own experiences in this matter is not commonly thought to be more persuasive than any other completely personal observation. 'You have seen fairies – or UFOs – but that doesn't prove there are any.' But Dom Illtyd's observation was not based on one incident or another, but a whole life's experience and testing. The invisible, the unobvious, the unnoticed by the world, all that is the subject and the object of faith. However, faith is God's gift, as God speaks to us and acts for us in his Son and in his Holy Spirit, enabling us to recognize his voice and his presence (Matthew 16:17); but we must hold by the gift and allow it to enlighten us, by cooperating with the grace that is given us. Otherwise we will stop still, stuck in misunderstanding (Matthew 16:22), or in danger of turning away from him (John 6:60, 66).

How can we avoid that? Since the objects of faith are beyond our sight, and the cares and diversions of this world can so easily make us forget them, we need to commit ourselves to them regularly in prayer and thought, so as to live as people who see them, and set our heart on them and our treasure in them.

I know the one in whom I have put my trust. (2 Timothy 1:12-14).

MEDITATING DAY AND NIGHT ON THE LAW OF THE LORD AND KEEPING VIGIL IN PRAYER

Carmelite reflections on Lectio Divina – the prayerful reading of the Bible

Carlos Mesters, O.Carm.
(translated by Míceál O'Neill, O.Carm.)

Each one of you is to stay in his own cell or nearby, pondering the Lord's law day and night and keeping watch at his prayers…
(Carmelite Rule: Chapter 10).

Lectio Divina *('holy reading/listening') is the ancient method of prayerfully reading the Bible, the Word of God. Originally cultivated by monastic orders – but now an important part of the lives of many Christians from different traditions – lectio divina enables us to contemplate God and God's will in our lives. If prayed regularly, lectio can deepen our relationship with God.*

A prayerful reading of the Bible within what is tradition-ally called *lectio divina* is an urgent task if we are to be faithful to what God asks of us today. It is something like curing the veins when the blood which keeps us alive has to flow. To this end, we offer:

- Ten words of advice about the 'mystical' life which must guide our prayerful reading of the Bible; that is, the light which needs to be in our eyes when we do our *lectio divina*. In these words of advice, reference is made to the *Carmelite Rule*, written by Saint Albert of Jerusalem in the early thirteenth century (the paragraph numbering follows that agreed by the Carmelite and Discalced Carmelite Orders in 1999).

- Ten points of orientation (the least possible) for personal and daily reading of the Bible (each person will gradu-ally develop his or her own way of communicating with the Word of God).

- Seven suggestions for reading the Word of God in groups; in these there is a reflection of the tradition of the 'four steps' of *Lectio Divina*.

The Process of *Lectio Divina*

1. When you begin a *lectio divina* of the Bible you are
    not concerned with study; you are not going to read
    the Bible in order either to increase your knowledge or
    to prepare for some apostolate. You are not reading
    the Bible in order to have some extraordinary experi-
    ence. You are going to read the Word of God in order
    to *listen* to what God has to say to you, to know his
    will and thus 'to live more deeply in allegiance to Je-
    sus Christ' (*Carmelite Rule: Chapter 2*). There must
    be poverty in you; you must also have the disposition
    which the old man Eli recommended to Samuel: 'Speak,
    Lord, your servant is listening' (*1 Samuel 3:10*).

2. Listening to God does not depend on you or on the ef-
    fort you make. It depends entirely on God, on God's
    freely-made decision to come into dialogue with you
    and to allow you to listen to the voice to God. Thus
    you need to *prepare yourself by asking him to send his
    Spirit*, since without the Spirit of God it is impossible
    to discover the meaning of the Word which God has
    prepared for us today (cf. *John 14:26*; *16:13*; *Lk
    11:13*).

3. It is important to *create the right surroundings* which
    will facilitate recollection and an attentive listening to
    the Word of God. For this, you must build your cell
    within you and around you and you must stay in it
    (*Carmelite Rule: Chapters 6 & 10*), all the time of
    your *lectio divina*. Putting one's body in the right po-
    sition helps recollection in the mind.

4. When you open the Bible, you have to be conscious
    that you are opening a Book which is not yours. It be-
    longs to *the community*. In your *lectio divina* you are
    setting foot in the great Tradition of the Church which
    has come down through the centuries. Your prayerful
    reading is like the ship which carries down the wind-

ing river to the sea. The light shining from the sea has already enlightened the dark night of many generations. In having your own experience of *lectio divina* you are alone. You are united to brothers and sisters who before you succeeded in 'meditating day and night upon the Law of the Lord and keeping vigil in prayer' (*Carmelite Rule: Chapter 10*).

5. An attentive and fruitful reading of the Bible involves three steps. It has to be marked from beginning to end, by three attitudes:

First Step/Attitude – Reading: First of all, you have to ask, *What does the text say as text?* This requires you to *be silent*. Everything in you must be silent so that nothing stands in the way of your gleaning what the texts say to you (*Carmelite Rule: Chapter 21*) and so that you do not make the text say what you would like to hear.

Second Step/Attitude – Meditation: You must ask, *What does the text say to me or to us?* In this second step we enter into *dialogue* with the text so that its meaning comes across with freshness and penetrates the life of the Carmelite today. Like Mary you will ponder what you have heard and 'meditate on the Law of the Lord' (*Carmelite Rule: Chapter 10*). In this way 'the Word of God will dwell abundantly on your lips and in your heart (*Carmelite Rule: Chapter 19*).

Third Step/Attitude – Prayer: Furthermore, you have to try to discover *What does the text lead me to say to God?* This is the moment of *prayer*, the moment of 'keeping watch in prayer' (*Carmelite Rule: Chapter 10*).

6. The result, the fourth step, the destination of *lectio divina*, is *contemplation*. Contemplation means having in one's eyes something of the 'wisdom which

leads to salvation' (*2 Timothy 3:15*). We begin to see the world and life through the eyes of the poor, through the eyes of God. We assume our own poverty and eliminate from our way of thinking all that smacks of the powerful. We recognise all the many things which we thought were fidelity to God, to the Gospel, and to the Tradition; in reality they were nothing more than fidelity to ourselves and our own interests. We get a taste, even now, of the love of God which is above all things. We come to see that in our lives true love of God is revealed in love of our neighbour (*Carmelite Rule: Chapters 15 & 19*). It is like saying always 'let it be done according to your Word' (*Luke 1:38*). Thus 'all you do will have the Lord's word for accompaniment' (*Carmelite Rule: Chapter 19*).

7. So that your *lectio divina* does not end up being the conclusions of your own feelings, thoughts and caprices, but has the deepest roots, it is important to take account of *three demands*:

    First Demand: *Check* the result of your reading *with the community* to which you belong (*Carmelite Rule: Chapter 15*), with the faith of the living Church. Otherwise it could happen that your effort might lead you nowhere (cf. *Galatians 2:2*).

    Second Demand: *Check* what you read in the Bible *with what is going on in life around you*. It was in confronting their faith with the situation existing around them that the people of God created the traditions which up to today are visible in the Bible. The desire to embody the contemplative ideal of the Carmelite Order within the reality of 'minores' (the poor of each age) brought the first Carmelite hermits to become mendicants among the people. When the *lectio divina* does not reach its goal in our life, the reason is not always our failure to pray, our lack of attention to the faith of the Church, or our lack of serious study of the text. Oftentimes it is simply our failure to pay attention to the crude and naked reality which surrounds us. The early Christian writer Cassian tells us that anyone who lives superficially – without seeking to go deeper – will not be able to reach the source where the Psalms were born.

Third Demand: *Check* the conclusions of your reading *with the results of biblical studies* which have shown the literal meaning of the words. *Lectio divina*, it has to be said, cannot remain chained to the letter. The Spirit's meaning has to be sought (*2 Corinthians 3:6*). However, any effort to identify the Spirit's meaning without basing it in the written word would be like trying to build a castle on sand (St. Augustine). That would be a way of falling into the trap of fundamentalism. In this day and age, when so many ideas are flying about, common sense is a most important quality. Common sense will be nourished by critical study of the written word. So that we will not go astray on this point, the Carmelite Rule tells us to follow the example of the Apostle Paul (*Carmelite Rule: Chapter 24*).

8. The Apostle Paul gives various bits of advice on how to read the Bible. He himself was an excellent interpreter. Here are some of the norms and attitudes which he taught and followed:

When you set yourself to read the Bible…

(a) *Look upon yourself as the one to whom the word is addressed*, since everything was written for our instruction (*1 Corinthians 10:11*; *Roman 15:4*). The Bible is *our* book.

(b) *Keep faith in Jesus Christ in your eyes*, since it is only through faith in Jesus Christ that the veil is removed and the Scripture reveals its meaning and tells of that wisdom which leads to salvation (*2 Corinthians 3:16*; *2 Timothy 3:15*; *Romans 15:4*).

(c) Remember how Paul spoke of 'Jesus Christ Crucified' (*2 Corinthians 2:2*), a 'stumbling block for some and foolishness for others'. It was this Jesus who opened Paul's eyes to see how, among the poor on the outskirts of Corinth, the foolishness and the stumbling block of the cross was confounding the wise, the strong, and those who believed themselves to be something in this world (*1 Corinthians 1:21-31*).

(d) *Unite 'I' and 'We'*: It is never a question of 'I' alone or 'We' alone. The Apostle Paul also united the two. He received his mission from the community of Antioch and spoke from that background (*Acts 13:1-3*).

(e) *Keep life's problems in mind*, that is, all that is happening in the Carmelite Family, in the communities, in the Church, and among the people to which you belong and whom you serve. Paul began from what was going on in the communities which he founded (*1 Corinthians 10:1-13*).

9. When you read the Bible, be always aware that the text of the Bible is not only a fact. It is also a *symbol* (*Hebrews 11:19*). It is both a window through which you see what happened to others in the past and *a mirror in which you can see what is happening to you today* (*1 Corinthians 10:6-10*). A prayerful reading is like a gentle flood which, little by little, waters the earth and makes it fruitful (*Isaiah 55:10-11*). In beginning to dialogue with God in *lectio divina*, you grow like a tree planted near streams of water (*Psalm 1:3*). You cannot see the growth but you can see its results in your encounter with yourself, with God, and with others. The song says: 'Like a flood that washes clean, like a fire that devours, so is your Word, leaving its mark upon me each time it passes'.

10. One final point to be born in mind: When you do a *lectio divina*, the principal object is not to interpret the Bible, nor to get to know its content, nor to increase your knowledge of the history of the people of God, nor to experience extraordinary things, but rather to *discover, with the help of the written Word, the living Word which God speaks to you today*, in your life, in our lives, in the life of the people, in the world in which we live (*Psalm 97:5*). The purpose is to grow in faith, like the prophet Elijah, and to experience more and more that 'the Lord lives, and I stand in his presence' (*1 Kings 17:1; 18:15*).

Ten points for personal *Lectio Divina*

The attitude of the faithful disciple:

The Lord God has given me the tongue of those who are taught, that I may know how to sustain with a word the one that is weary. Morning by morning God wakens, wakens my ear to hear as those who are taught. (*Isaiah 50:4*).

1. Opening prayer: an invocation of the Holy Spirit
2. Slow and attentive reading of the text
3. A moment of interior silence, to recall what I have read
4. Look at the meaning of each phrase
5. Bring the word into the present, ponder it in relation to my life
6. Broaden my vision by relating this text to other biblical texts
7. Read the text again, prayerfully, giving a response to God
8. Formulate my commitment in life
9. Pray a suitable psalm
10. Choose a phrase which captures the meaning and memorise it

The Lord God has opened my ear, and I was not rebellious, I turned not backward. I gave my back to the smiters... For the Lord God helps me; therefore I have set my face like a flint, and I know that I shall not be put to shame; he who vindicates me is near. (Isaiah 50:5-8).

Seven suggestions for group *Lectio Divina*

Jesus stood in their midst and said: Peace be with you. Then he opened their minds to understand the scriptures. (Luke 24:36, 45).

And Jesus said: the Holy Spirit, whom the Father will send in my name, will teach you all things, and bring to your remembrance all that 1 have said to you ... the Spirit will guide you into all the truth. (John 14:26; 16:13).

1. **Welcome and prayer**
   - A word of welcome and of sharing expectations.
   - Opening prayer, asking for the light of the Holy Spirit.

2. **Reading of the text**
   - Slow and attentive reading, followed by a moment of silence.
   - Remaining silent, allowing the Word to come.
   - Repeating the text by asking each one to recall a word or phrase from it, until the whole text is heard again.

3. **What does the text say?**
   - Share impressions and questions as to what the text is saying.
   - If necessary, read the text again and help one another to understand it.
   - A moment of silence in order to assimilate all that has been heard.

4. **Its meaning for us**
   - Ponder the text and discover its meaning for today.
   - Apply the meaning of the text to the situation in which we live today.
   - Broaden the meaning, by relating this text to the other texts in the Bible.

- Situate the text in God's plan which is accomplished in human history.

5. **Pray with the text**
   - Read the text again with great attention.
   - A moment of silence in order to prepare our response to God.
   - Share, in the form of intercessions, the lights and strengths which have been received.

6. **Contemplation and commitment**
   - Formulate the commitment to which the prayerful reading has led.
   - Choose a phrase which captures the whole message in order to take that phrase with you throughout the day.

7. **A psalm**
   - Pick a psalm which is in tune with all that has been experienced in the meeting.
   - Conclude the meeting by reciting the psalm.

And when they heard it, they lifted their voices together to God and said, 'Sovereign Lord, who made the heaven and the earth and the sea and everything in them, who by the mouth of our father David, your servant, said by the Holy Spirit, 'Why did the Gentiles rage, and the peoples imagine vain things? The kings of the earth set themselves in array and the rulers were gathered together, against the Lord and against his Anointed.'... And now Lord, look upon their threats, and grant to your servant to speak your word with all boldness...' And when they had prayed, the place in which they were gathered together was shaken; and they were all filled with the Holy Spirit and spoke the word of God with boldness. (Acts 4:24-26, 29, 31).

The Carmelite Family in Britain

The Order of Carmelites, or Brethren of the Blessed Virgin Mary of Mount Carmel developed from a group of hermits, priests and lay-people living a contemplative life modelled on Elijah and the Virgin Mary, in twelfth-century Palestine. By the year 1214 we had received our *Rule of Life* from St. Albert, Patriarch of Jerusalem. We first came to Britain in 1242. As the hermits became friars following the 1247 General Chapter in Aylesford, and later in 1452 when nuns and lay-people were formally admitted to the Order, the Carmelites developed their distinctive mission of following in the footsteps of Jesus by forming communities for prayer and for the service of local people. The heart of the Carmelite vocation is contemplation, that is, pondering God and God's will in our lives.

The British Isles boasted the largest Carmelite Province in the Order until its suppression at the Reformation. The British Province was re-established under the patronage of Our Lady of the Assumption in the twentieth century. There are currently six communities of friars, three of sisters and many local groups of Lay Carmelites in England, Scotland, and Wales. Similar communities exist in Ireland, and Discalced Carmelites are also present in the British Isles. Members of the Carmelite Family seek the face of the Living God in parishes, prisons, university chaplaincies, retreat centres, workplaces, and through many other forms of ministry.

**Further sources of information
on Carmelite spirituality include:**

John Welch, O.Carm.,
The Carmelite Way: An Ancient Path for Today's Pilgrim,
(Leominster: Gracewing, 1996).

Wilfrid McGreal, O.Carm.,
At the Fountain of Elijah: The Carmelite Tradition,
(London: Darton, Longman and Todd, 1999).

Website of the British Province of Carmelites
www.carmelite.org

For further titles on Carmelite spirituality, please contact:

The Friars Bookshop
The Friars
Aylesford
Kent
ME20 7BX
U.K.

☎ + 44 (01622) 715770

E-mail: bookshop@thefriars.org.uk

http://www.carmelite.org